KICKING
THE COFFEE*
HABIT

BOOKS BY CHARLES F. WETHERALL

Quit: Read This Book And Stop Smoking Forever

Diet: Read This Book And Stay Slim Forever

KICKING
THE COFFEE*
HABIT

———

CHARLES F. WETHERALL

EDITED BY JUDY GALBRAITH

———

Wetherall Publishing Company
Minneapolis

To the 15,000,000 coffee addicts in the U.S. who are hooked on a bum drug — and may not even know it.

Contents

Introduction

Not long ago, I was a coffee drinker of the first magnitude, a true coffee addict. Not more than 10 minutes after I had raised my groggy head from the pillow, a cup of coffee was in my hand. And not more than 15 minutes before I plopped that hopped up head back on the pillow at night, I had polished off maybe my 10th or 15th cup of the day. In the hours between was a daylong, handle-holding embrace with the drug of my "choice," Coffea arabica.

I was hooked not so much because of the *amount* of coffee I drank, which was considerable, but because of what coffee was *doing to me*, some of which I was largely unaware, and all of which I seemed helpless to change.

It wasn't always like that. In high school my coffee drinking was occasional and moderate; beer was more the drink of the day. Even in college, although I drank coffee more or less regularly each day, my consumption was still limited to what might be called moderate proportions: two or three cups a day.

But after college when I joined the work force, a job brought stability not only to my life, but also to my coffee drinking.

Coffee, like the popular song says, "got me going" to my 9 to 5 as a newspaper and television reporter, later as a public relations executive and then as an author.

As the years passed, my coffee intake gradually escalated until my drinking assumed addictive proportions and predictability: at least two cups to get me out the door of my house (more if I had been partying the night before), a cup as I drove to work, about three or four cups at work in the morning, maybe two or three cups in the afternoon. A heavy schedule of meetings might double the number. Working out of the office and away from the coffeepot might halve the quota.

In all, I was probably averaging about 10 to 12 cups a day. On weekends, my intake dropped considerably. Maybe I'd drink only 10 cups all weekend.

Though I occasionally drank coffee in the evening, it always tasted best in the morning. Without it, as a matter of fact, I didn't believe I could operate.

Does this scenario sound familiar? It should. It is happening to millions of Americans—and probably to you.

For many years I continued my coffee drinking habits, never giving it much thought at all. I can't remember ever reading any newspaper or magazine articles about the evils of coffee drinking; I never heard about it on radio or TV. Or if I did, I must have immediately forgotten about it.

I had few complaints about the way I felt each day, or about my health in general. Yes, I felt a little logy on some mornings, but I reasoned that was because I "didn't sleep too well" or it was something I ate. I had a few sleepless nights.

Otherwise, I was right in there with the millions of coffee heads who drink their drugs, accept whatever small misfortunes the chemicals may bring, and who argue inexhaustibly that coffee is the A-OK, all-American drink, and that those who accuse it of being harmful are health nuts or just nuts in general.

For many coffee drinkers, coffee is not an addiction. They can drink a cup or two of coffee a day and that's it. No problem. But for millions of other coffee drinkers, it doesn't end at a cup or two. Two becomes three. Three becomes four. Until we're drinking coffee *despite* its harmful effects, and maybe even *because* of them. It's at this point we're out of control whether we know it or not. We're hooked, trapped like some 15,000,000 other souls by a drug that dictates how we live, when we live, and even perhaps *if* we live. Coffee controls our lives.

The Beginning of the End

It all began with a shiny little coffee maker. I was interviewing a real estate executive in his office and he offered me a cup of coffee. I declined the coffee because it gets in the way of good note-taking, but I was fascinated by the little gizmo he was making it in. We talked at length about it.

His coffee maker was a little stainless steel cup with a wide brim on the bottom. It sat atop the cup in which he was going to make (and drink) his coffee. First, he unscrewed a saucer-shaped plunger from within the gadget (I later learned it was just a coffee filter), then he added a couple spoonfuls of coffee and replaced the plunger, turning it tightly to compress the load. Finally, he poured a bit of water into the shiny cup, unscrewed the plunger a bit more, and then poured the remainder through the filter.

Voilà! In just four or five minutes, he had made himself a real gourmet cup of coffee that I was sure tasted superior to anything Mrs. Olson had ever dreamed of. So sure of this was I, that the very next day I had one of these little beauties in my office. That, plus gourmet coffee beans at $6 or so a pound, a coffee grinder (so I could grind my coffee fresh each day, or sometimes, fresh each *cup*), a fancy new mug, and a whole new (and superior) attitude about coffee drinking. Not only would I be drinking a better cup of coffee, I reasoned, I also would be drinking less of it (a growing concern of mine) because this thing makes getting a cup of coffee a major undertaking.

During this whole period, I was working extremely long and hard hours—always seven days a week and usually every night as well. And boy, did I drink coffee. I drank coffee all day long and for the first time well into the night. Oddly enough, the coffee never disturbed my sleep, for which I was both thankful and mystified.

But fate fooled me. Instead of drinking *less* coffee, my intake was rapidly escalating. I was now drinking about 12-16 cups a day, all day long. And I also was drinking potfuls on the weekends, to keep me company as I worked hour after hour.

How I put up with that nuisance is beyond me. Heating fresh water all the time. Mixing those little cups of coffee. Cleaning up those little coffee grounds messes from my credenza, from the carpeting, from my desk, and often from important papers. I must have really loved my coffee. Or did I?

Perhaps that was the important thing about that silly little coffee filter and the tedious, time consuming chore of making coffee by the cupful. No, it didn't reduce my coffee consumption one ounce. But it did make me startlingly aware of how much of that thick, black junk (and I really made it black) I was pouring into my body and I grew worried about the effect.

Like millions of other Americans, I had become more health-conscious in recent years and I was concerned about all the junk that I was giving my mind and body to live on. I had already forsworn alcohol and cigarettes. I had substantially reduced my sugar intake.

But don't get me wrong, though, I wasn't a "health nut." I didn't know the first thing about whole grains, bean sprouts or yogurt. I was just trying to feel decent and keep my body together as best I knew how. Coffee was the black mark, however, on an otherwise healthy record of diet and nutrition. And I was slowly becoming aware of what millions of other Americans had already learned: coffee does absolutely nothing *good* for you; and worse, it can get your body in a whole lot of trouble.

I learned that in a most painful sort of way. Like most coffee drinkers, I endured a certain amount of discomfort directly related to my coffee drinking. The occasional sleepless nights. The stomach pains. The hyper feeling after I swilled down several cups. But most of the discomforts were short-lived. I couldn't see any sort of permanent injury growing out of its use.

But then one day a different truth became known: everything was "fine"—*only so long as I had my drug*. The jig was up when I didn't. And one day I didn't.

I had run out of coffee at my office and was too busy to get some. No matter. But I hadn't had any coffee since the previous day and now, under a heavy workload, I deeply craved a cup. Within hours, a headache swept over my skull like you wouldn't believe. I don't ordinarily get headaches so I don't keep aspirin. I was just stuck. And this really was a whopper of a headache. Then came the sweaty palms, the nervousness, the nausea; I could hardly type. I really didn't know what was going on with me.

"Could all of this be happening because I'm not drinking coffee," I wondered? "This is terrible," I thought. "I've got to get out of here. I've got to have a cup of coffee."

I left my office and took the elevator downstairs to a newsstand that sells smoking goods, soda, and most importantly, coffee. They serve the stuff in those white Styrofoam cups, so you know it's plenty black and it's awful. And it was. But within 10 to 15 minutes, after I had guzzled the coffee like a skid row alcoholic, I felt a good deal better and was able to dig back into my work.

I made several more trips downstairs to get coffee, in what turned out to be a daylong review of my coffee drinking habits. You know how things can sometimes really prey on your mind? Much as you try to think about other things, the unwanted subject just keeps popping back into your head. Well, my day turned into one of those cerebral wrestling matches, an all day confrontation of my coffee drinking habits. I began to add things up a whole new way. I was forced to realize some disagreeable facts.

What the hell is going on here? Who's running things? The answers were obvious. This habit was leading me around by my nose. *I* wasn't in charge at all. This drug caffeine, or coffee, was telling me *how* I would spend my mornings, *when* I would leave for work, when I had to rush back to the pot for another fix. Coffee sent me to the store to "stock up" on my drug, just like an alcoholic.

And the weird part about it was that I didn't really like coffee. Sure, I liked *some* of the coffee that I drank. Certainly, the first cup or two in the morning were good. So were those following meals. But what about all those cups in between? I had been drinking those without much taste or satisfaction. . . they were drank in sheer addiction, and out of mindless habit.

It was like that when I used to smoke cigarettes. There were a few cigarettes that I really enjoyed, like the ones following my meals (and usually with a cup of coffee), or those when I sat down and relaxed. But beyond that, I was smoking cigarette after cigarette without an ounce of satisfaction.

Not only was I most certainly the victim of a hellish habit, I reasoned, but the addiction was causing me to suffer in ways which I was only now willing to take a good look at. How many grouchy days have I endured which were caused by coffee? How many stomachaches were caused by this drug? What about that hyper feeling, that nervousness and anxiety? Were they linked with my coffee habit? And God knows what else coffee is doing to me.

Sure, I've heard other people complain about what coffee did to their systems, but I hadn't *really thought* about what it was doing to mine. I just *assumed* that when I felt crummy it was because I hadn't eaten breakfast, or I stayed out late the night before, or I just hadn't slept well. Nobody knows how I would have behaved all these years had I *not* been drinking coffee. Nobody knows what's in store for me now — Cancer? Heart disease? Ulcers? Premature death?

The list of ailments which I thought to be associated with my coffee drinking grew and grew. But I had absolutely no idea whether they were, in fact, the *cause* of the problems which had now become so clear. And there was only one way to find out.

That's when I said, out loud, "I've had it. Enough is enough."

And so I quit. Cold turkey. It wasn't easy, at first. There were the powerful, pounding headaches that hung on for days. The irritability. The funny stomach. The tremendous preoccupation. True withdrawal in every sense of the word.

But after about a week and I had cleared my system, a number of interesting things happened. First, I felt a great deal better. That funny logy feeling I'd get after drinking a great deal of coffee vanished. And what I found out was that I really hadn't known what a good night's sleep was all about. I only *thought* I knew. Likewise, I had always perceived myself as a calm, easygoing sort but when I quit drinking, friends and associates remarked how much calmer, and easygoing I was (and here I thought I had been that way all along).

Gone was the sour feeling I had frequently experienced in my stomach and never knew who or what to blame. Usually I blamed that on the fact that I'd had no breakfast.

Like other former coffee drinkers the world over, I had struck out for a healthier, more enjoyable life without coffee—the result of self-diagnosis and self-prescription of the highest order.

Later I was to learn that there are millions more like me, who, without the benefit of a well-publicized anti-coffee campaign, had made our own decision about our own bodies.

For the truth about coffee is both easy and difficult to discover, I was to learn. Yes, there are a number of important studies by respected doctors, famous hospitals and universities and independent researchers which indict coffee as being both causally related to, and associated with, a wide variety of pathological illnesses. But where are these reports? They are virtually hidden away in obscure medical journals, government bulletins, and foundation memos where few physicians and fewer coffee drinkers can assimilate the totality of the prognosis.

Yet the truth is easy to discover *if you ask the coffee drinkers themselves* about what coffee is doing to their minds and their bodies. That's what I did. Here, the evidence is incontrovertible. The coffee drinkers, and particularly the *former* coffee drinkers, know the truth: Coffee Drinking Is America's #1 Drug Threat.

We interviewed more than 200 men and women who had "kicked the habit"—men and women just like yourself who had become suspicious about what coffee was doing to their minds and their bodies.

They came in all ages. Some were as young as 19 years old. One was 80 years old. But most of the subjects in our study were in their middle years, somewhere between 30 and 55 years old.

Their addictive habits were spread over a number of years. While many had been addictively drinking coffee for just a year or two, the majority of "quitters" had been habitual coffee users for anywhere from 10 to 30 years before they decided they were fed up with this hazardous dependency.

Surprisingly, their addictive consumption levels also differed markedly. Some were "hooked" on just three or four cups of coffee per day. Others had built up habits which required 10, 15 or even 20 cups a day to satisfy.

Despite their differences in age, occupation, sex, income, level of consumption and a number of other variables, they shared in common their addiction to coffee. And they were eager to tell their stories so that others may learn—and live.

Thus, this book brings together, perhaps for the first time, the most relevant of the vast array of studies on coffee and caffeine use, and the stories from the coffee addicts themselves.

Their testimonies are, by far, the most important part of "Kicking the Coffee Habit." The doctors, clinicians and research authorities are now coming to a consensus that coffee and caffeine are dangerous to your health. But it likely will be years before the final exchange in the controversial battle has been completed. . . and years before the final indictment has been issued.

In the meantime, the public suffers. *But not everybody.*

Millions of former coffee drinkers are wise to the ills which this drug can produce. Their horror stories may at times frighten you, but they will also, I hope, enlighten. Once you read their stories, you're likely to be struck with the realization that *their* experiences are *your* experiences. And together, I hope this book will convince you to start a new life for yourself, a healthier life. I hope that you'll kick the coffee habit today!

1

Coffee: America's #1 Drug Habit

Carol T. is a 37-year-old mother of two teenaged children whose life parallels that of millions of other mothers across the country. Active in church and busy in volunteer work, Carol still has time to be a productive mother and manager for her husband and pre-adult son and daughter. Her life is "normal" in most every respect. Except that Carol is a coffee addict.

She began her slip into coffee dependency when she was 17 years old, a high school senior at a small Minneapolis high school. Carol picked up the coffee habit from her family. She began young, just like her mother, father and her two brothers.

Her consumption was typical, too. At least, in the beginning. She normally had only a cup or two a day. Inevitably, she had an "eye-opener" in the morning. She'd have another about mid-morning at the office where she worked as a secretary.

That's how it is for many Americans. A cup or two a day. And that's it.

But for Carol and for a frightening number of other coffee drinkers, two cups was just the beginning. It was just a point along a coffee drinking continuum that leads to addictive use. Soon, Carol was drinking three cups a day. Then four. Then five, six and seven. And in just four short years, she was drinking coffee at levels which all medical authorities would agree is harmful to your health: 18 cups a day.

By the time Carol was married and 23 years old, she was experiencing severe headaches, hypertension and a variety of central nervous system disorders that often made her life miserable.

Sometimes her hands and face would become puffy and "very tender" to the touch. Frequently her breasts would become "lumpy and quite painful", particularly when she was approaching her menstrual period. She suffered from nausea and frequent stomach pains.

Carol was both frightened of and alarmed at these unexplained physical and mental disorders. But because they came and went, she didn't see her doctor. Instead, each time they came, she endured the extremely painful discomforts. And each time they went, she hoped she had seen their last.

But she didn't.

But the time she was 29, the headaches had reached such intensity and frequency, she visited her family physician, who in turn, referred her to a neurologist. Brain scans were taken. Batteries of physical and psychological tests were given. But no answers were forthcoming. Her headaches, however, were unremitting. Her doctor finally hospitalized her for still more tests. Even an angiogram showed nothing. The doctor, she said, was completely baffled by her case.

But Carol wasn't. She told the doctor that her problem must have something to do with her diet, and suggested it might well have something to do with her coffee consumption. The doctor reluctantly agreed with her diagnosis and with her self-prescription: Quit Drinking Coffee.

At first, it was extremely difficult. Carol suffered headaches even worse than the explosive head-breakers she had previously endured. She continued to be sick to her stomach. But after a few days, the headaches disappeared. She felt a great burst of energy, her own *natural* energy, the kind she left behind in youthful days. She slept much better. Gone were the lumps in her breasts, the puffy hands and face, and that "hyper" feeling.

Carol has kicked the habit. She has freed herself from the persistent, on-going miseries that inevitably accompany addictive coffee use. While she may still suffer from deadly pathologies, as a part of the long-term outlook for coffee addicts, she is at least, temporarily free. And she is certainly not alone.

The Coffee Junkies

Millions of Americans like Carol are hooked on coffee, risking dozens of health hazards—many of them fatal. They "need" their drug just as surely as smokers become *absolutely dependent* on a daily dose of cigarettes. Their chemical withdrawal can be just as painful and even more long-lasting than that of the most chronic alcoholic. And just like all junkies, this dependence strips them of their freedom. They give up their minds, their bodies, and even their lives, to the debilitating drug of their "choice": coffee.

Coffee, and its powerfully addictive agent, caffeine, are wrecking a pathological war on this country which is potentially as ruinous as it is now widespread. Yet few Americans, and shockingly fewer doctors, realize that coffee and caffeine may well be the most significant drug threat of our times. The significance is amply demonstrated by its widespread use and abuse, and by the plethora of physiologic and psychotropic illnesses—and even death—coffee and caffeine visit upon an often naive and unknowing public. Not only are millions hooked on coffee, but most of them don't even know it, so insidious is its addictive onslaught.

The Double-Barreled Threat

Let us be perfectly clear at the outset about the deadly culprits that we are indicting. We are talking about two separate but related chemical compounds; one, a component of the other. Individually and in concert, they present a clear and present danger to an American people who are abusing these substances in record numbers.

We are talking about *caffeine*, the drug which occurs naturally in coffee, tea, cocoa, and chocolate and which is widely and unwisely used to adulterate soft drinks, foods and medicines.

We also are talking about *coffee*—regardless of whether it contains caffeine or not. Caffeine is responsible for one constellation of illnesses; coffee is responsible for quite another. Together, they pose the Number One drug threat in a country where its abuse is the *rule*, rather than the exception.

Drug Use in America

Certainly, there are other drugs which are almost as widely *used* than coffee. Alcohol, for example, is reported to be used by some 75,000,000 Americans. Despite its widespread use, however, there are only an estimated 9,000,000 alcoholics.

Likewise, it could be argued that some drugs *may* produce more deaths and more readily apparent disease—both mental and physical—than coffee addiction.

But coffee is absolutely Public Health Enemy Number One when measured along several significant continuums. There are more coffee drug addicts in the U.S. than drug addicts of any other kind. There is no other addiction which so completely permeates the fabric of American life—and yet we profess to know so little about. And lastly, there is no other addiction which has been the object of so few campaigns to erase it from the American scene.

Table 1. Reported Drug Use by American Youth and Adults for Nonmedical Purposes

	Youth (Ages 12-17)		Adults (18 and Over)	
	Per-cent	Population	Per-cent	Population
Coffee	7.9	1,540,000	55.2	98,837,596
Alcoholic beverages	24	5,977,200	53	74,080,220
Tobacco, cigarettes	17	4,233,850	38	53,114,120
Proprietary sedatives, tranquilizers, stimulants	6	1,494,300	7	9,784,180
Ethical sedatives	3	747,150	4	5,590,960
Ethical tranquilizers	3	747,150	6	8,386,440
Ethical stimulants	4	996,200	5	6,988,700
Marijuana	14	3,486,700	16	22,363,840
LSD, other hallucinogens	4.8	1,195,440	4.6	6,429,604
Glue, other inhalants	6.4	1,593,920	2.1	2,935,254
Cocaine	1.5	373,575	3.2	4,472,768
Heroin	.6	149,430	1.3	1,817,062

Source: Adapted from study by National Commission on Marijuana and Drug Abuse

What Doctors Tell Us

Ask any doctor about how much coffee you can safely drink and you'll likely be told about a cup or two per day. Medical authorities and researchers are almost universal in their agreement that ingesting anything more than a couple of cups of coffee per day is asking for medical problems. *Moderation* is the key word. And moderation, as we all know, means nothing in America.

Moderation is the *exception,* rather than the rule for most coffee drinkers. According to figures provided by the National Coffee Association of the U.S.A., Inc., American coffee drinkers average 3.56 cups per day.[1] In some sections of the country, coffee drinkers *average* over *four* cups per day. In other words, we're a nation of coffee drinkers who consume *on the average,* anywhere from 1-1/2 to 4 times what our own doctors and clinicians tell us is safe.

Let me repeat that. The *average* American coffee drinker is drinking anywhere from 1-1/2 to 4 times more coffee each day than medical good sense tells us is acceptable. And that's the *average*.

Millions of Americans are drinking a great deal *more* than the average. It was easy for our researchers to find coffee drinkers who polish off 10, 15, 20 even up to 50 cups of coffee a day!

And professional researchers readily confirm what our informal survey revealed: Americans are hooked on coffee more than ever before. A government study shows that at least 68,240,000 Americans drink three cups of coffee or more each day. At least 30,000,000 drink at least *five* cups a day or more. And some 21,000,000 drink six or more cups of coffee a day.[2]

Thus, the gravity of the problem is as shocking as it is enormous. At least 45,000,000 people drink coffee in amounts that *greatly exceed* doctor-recommended levels. At least 15,000,000 people in America drink coffee excessively—*and addictively*.[3] Millions more abuse caffeine-containing beverages, thereby doubling, tripling or even quadrupling their exposure to illness and disease.

The mental and physical wounds from these addictions staggers the imagination. They are so enormous, in fact, that the full extent of the American coffee/caffeine addiction is only beginning to become manifest.

Coffee—A Most Insidious Drug

What makes caffeine and coffee so dangerous is the insidious manner in which they work their destructive ways. Unlike alcohol and hard drugs which produce a dramatic and almost instant pathological response, coffee is quite innocent—at least in the beginning. And, it is just this commonality that betrays us. How can something so ubiquitous as coffee be harmful to your health?

We've grown up with coffee all around us. It flows easily and widely in virtually every home, restaurant, hospital, hotel and church in the country. It is the eye-opener of the world, the great social lubricant, the All-American beverage at meal and break times, the universal elixir of klatches and college study halls. We have *assumed* it to be safe precisely because it is so common, so much a part of the American fabric. How could something so widely used, we reason, be harmful to our health? Can 100 million coffee drinkers be wrong?

The nettlesome truth, however, is that the ubiquitous cigarette also was once considered harmless. So was DDT, countless over-the-counter drugs and a vast number of chemicals which we have used so freely, so frequently before we knew their true potential. But then, new discoveries were made. Years of research provoked oftentimes bitter controversy. And then the truth of these compounds was revealed. They were found to be far more harmful than we at first believed; they were found to be extremely dangerous to life itself. Unfortunately, we all too often learned too little, too late.

From Innocent Beginnings

Coffee drinkers begin the precipitous descent from novice to addict innocently enough. For most Americans, the daily coffee habit begins routinely each day with a morning "eye-opener" of hardy, black coffee. This ritual which will be repeated once, perhaps twice during the day.

For thousands of years, we have praised coffee's ability to promote rapid and clear thinking, to improve intellectual effort, enhance mental acuity—all valued attributes in a society which worships success and achievement. How can something so *right*, then, be so *wrong?* Simple. The American way is: **More Is Better!**

Repeated once or twice, and we have the typical American coffee drinker who consumes a couple of cups each day without incident, without apparent complaint.

His habit usually begins in response to social or peer group pressure or as a part of family socialization. The vast majority of coffee drinkers who remain at low levels of a cup or two each day, have only occasional complaints: a sleepless night here; an unsettled stomach once in a while.

Most health authorities would agree that coffee consumption at levels of one or two cups a day poses no significant health hazard. But millions of coffee drinkers, like millions of cigarette smokers and alcohol drinkers, *don't stop* at just one or two. They go on and on and on—often with devastating results.

And who knows the reason why? Who knows why some drinkers become alcoholics and others remain "social" drinkers. Who can say why some people can experiment with drugs and leave them behind and others continue on making them a major and debilitating part of their lives?

The Secret Storm

Regardless of the reasons why, as intake begins to climb, so does the pain, the suffering, the illness and disease. Unfortunately, the buildup is often so slow that the causal relationship between coffee consumption and ill effects is difficult to define, or entirely lost.

Thus, the coffee addict becomes difficult to identify. That's because caffeine's toxic effect on the body is extremely variable from person to person. Some people are very susceptible to its toxic effects and others are not. Many factors account for this wide ranging variance, among them age, weight, metabolism, sex, and certainly, the degree of tolerance one has built up to the drug.

The American Way: More is Better

Tolerance is one of those double-edged swords inherent in most drug use, where the pharmacological effect of the drug becomes less significant over time. That's why increasingly larger doses are needed to obtain the same effect. And that's why heroin users build up $1,000-a-week habits; smokers shoot up a couple of packs a day; and coffee drinkers inject 5, 10 or even 25 or 30 cups a day.

Chronic coffee users who have built up a considerable tolerance to this drug find it extremely difficult to satisfy their craving for coffee with smaller doses. Conversely, coffee drinkers who have not built up a tolerance, the ingestion of caffeine in amounts as large as their fellow heavy coffee drinkers would undoubtedly send them so high, they'd suffer anywhere from tremors and jitteriness to delirium and hallucinations. Because heavy coffee drinkers have built up such a tremendous drug tolerance, they have fewer yardsticks to tell them when they're in trouble.

Yet the occasions for coffee abuse are everywhere—occurring millions of times each day with a regularity as predictable as rising suns and coffee breaks. The price we pay for these addictive abuses is staggering and made all the more so because the addict is not altogether aware that he or she is an unwitting victim.

Are You In Trouble?

Coffee addiction is not a matter of *how much* you drink, but rather, what effect whatever amount you drink has on your mind and body. And therein lies the problem: most coffee addicts don't really know they're addicts.

Some addicts cannot recognize in their mind or body the existence of pathological disturbances caused by coffee. Irritability and mood swings, for example, are often symptoms of coffee addiction. The addict himself may not recognize these symptoms, however, because the trait has for so long been a part of his personality. He believes his behavior is normal. Family and friends may also be oblivious to the relationship of coffee as a mood altering substance.

On the other hand, the addict may not relate a condition of which she *is* aware to her coffee intake, whether thought to be "excessive" or not. For example, the coffee abuser may realize that she has lumps in her breasts but is unaware that they may be related to her coffee intake.

Or, he can readily recognize a malady, and even link it with his coffee intake, but his addiction renders him unable or unwilling to do anything about it.

Many coffee drinkers report they suffer from severe stomach pains and they have reasonably strong beliefs that the discomfort may be caused by coffee consumption. But because they "enjoy" their coffee so much, they refuse to do anything about limiting their excessive consumption.

The situations above are not entirely unlike that of other drug addicts, particularly alcoholics. Many alcoholics are *unaware* they are alcoholic and they are equally unaware of what the drug is doing to their minds and bodies. Likewise, many alcoholics are aware of the problems associated with their drug use but will not, or cannot do anything about it. They are truly dependent.

Worse yet, both coffee drinkers and alcoholics share the need for self-protective armor: they tend to minimize both their intake and its effect on mind and body, a rationalization to help perpetuate the drug habit.

The Trouble With Coffee

Because caffeine is such a powerful stimulant, virtually the entire body is swept up into its control. While deaths from caffeine overdoses are rare—it is interesting to note that such overdoses can and do occur.

Depending on the amount consumed, caffeine users have been widely known to experience nervousness, headaches, tremulousness, visual flashes, hyperesthesia, insomnia, increased agitation and irritability. These symptoms of the central nervous system (CNS) overdose are so prevalent in our society that we have invented a name for them, "coffee nerves."

And if coffee nerves were all we had to cope with in our excessive coffee use, it would be disturbing enough. But there are a great many more, perhaps even fatal pathologies, lurking in the shadows of clinical research.

Take the heart, for example. Caffeine can create such a strain on the heart that it should be no surprise at all that heart disease has been linked to coffee consumption.

Caffeine's action on the cardiovascular system can be recorded in systemic, coronary and cerebral circulation patterns. Coronary arteries and the pulmonary and general systemic vessels become dilated following coffee ingestion, increasing the flow of blood to the heart muscle while *decreasing* the flow to the brain by constricting cerebral blood vessels. Then, any and all manner of abnormalities strike the heart.

Research has shown that abnormally fast heart beats occur (tachycardia), as well as slower than normal heart beats (bradycardia), extra contractions between heart beats (extra-systoles), irregular heart beats (arrhythmias), abnormally low blood pressure (hypotension) and abnormally high blood pressure (hypertension).

Still more abnormalities are evident in the gastrointestinal system, where we will reveal studies which show that coffee drinking is related to nausea, vomiting, diarrhea, epigastric pain, peptic ulcers, diuresis, and hematemesis, the vomiting of blood. And it appears that these ailments are prevalent whether the coffee you drink is regular *or* decaffeinated.

These are just a few of the *short-range* implications of coffee drinking on which we'll be elaborating. The prognosis for the long haul, the matter of life and death, is a picture that is growing ever more stark.

Coffee, as we shall see, has been accused with the incidence of heart disease, linked with cancer of the pancreas and bladder. It has also been linked with hypoglycemia, a low blood sugar ailment that strikes millions of Americans.

For women, children and seniors, another tale of pathological woe as research uncovers more and more diseases and ailments that are associated with these chemicals.

Women should be especially warned about the danger of fibrocystic breast tumors and breast cancer, possible birth defects in their children, stillbirths, miscarriages and more.

Children, because of their weight and the correspondingly greater effect of caffeine, are especially sensitive. Two or three colas are equal to an addictive level if taken every day. The elderly, more keenly aware of bodily disturbances, are often the victims of sleepless nights and jittery days because of coffee overdose. Coffee often works at cross-purposes with prescribed drugs. One drug may cancel the pharmacological effect of the other. The same problem has been reported in hospitals, clinics, mental wards and more.

The Grim Prognosis

As researchers turn their clinical gaze on coffee with keener, more knowledgeable eyes, more and more pathologies, some of them fatal, are likely to be inextricably linked with coffee consumption. The scenario will no doubt blaze the same trail as cigarette smoking did. It was first "associated" with, and then *proven* to be a major cause of cancer and heart disease.

Meanwhile, a public which is eager for the truth still waits and wants for information. They are undecided on a course of action. Some still believe that coffee is entirely safe and they'll continue to swill cup after cup, day after day. A growing number of Americans, however, are putting two and two together and are kicking the coffee habit altogether. In effect, they're far ahead of government and way out in front of researchers and medical authorities. They've come to believe, through their own self-diagnosis and subsequent self-prescription, that coffee drinking is dangerous to their health.

And they're going to be at the forefront of the Coffee Kicking movement, which is already well underway.

They're not health nuts. They're just people who recognized that coffee was doing a terrible number on their minds and bodies. They've decided to call it quits. I think after you read this book, you'll be ready to call it quits too.

2

Double Jeopardy

There is a tremendous lack of understanding among most Americans as to the focal point of the coffee controversy. Mention coffee consumption and related health problems and most people will instantly think about *caffeine*, as if this drug were entirely responsible for any and all ailments that coffee produces.

I suspect that part of that reason is the coffee industry's recent preoccupation with caffeine and the marketing of the newer, decaffeinated coffees.

All Robert Young talks about is those grouchy, temperamental, bellyaching souls who drink too much caffeinated coffee. We hear it so often from Young and others that we lose sight of the total picture.

Research shows that *both* coffee and caffeine can cause ill-health, although perhaps one more than the other.

Neither coffee nor caffeine is *good* for you. Nobody has ever suggested they are. None of the radio or TV commercials, and none of the ads you've seen extolling coffee ever said a single word about *nutritional* or even *psychological* benefits of drinking coffee. In true Madison Avenue method, the ads sell consumers the sizzle and not the steak. They talk in glowing terms about the taste, aroma and even *appearance* of coffee. But not a word about any *good* that coffee can do for you. And it's easy to see why. Coffee doesn't do anything good for you. The ultimate question is to assess the degree of damage that caffeine and coffee can cause.

Coffee, in addition to caffeine, contains a number of compounds. The physiological implications of few have been determined. Coffee contains trigonelline, chorogenic acid and tannic acid, a yellowish astringent substance which also is used in tanning leathers.[1]

Non-volatile acids in coffee include caffeic and quinic acids, plus some others which have not even been identified. Coffee contains volatile ingredients such as acetic, propionic, butyric and valeric acids. And there is furfural, acetoin, ketones and a variety of other acidic carbonyl compounds.[2]

These are the major components that occur naturally in coffee. Other compounds are added, subtracted, and even converted during the roasting and brewing processes, to further obscure coffee's true identity and pharmacological role. Thus, science has not put the finger on *exactly which* components in coffee produce what pathologies. The closest we can get is that research finds that both coffee *and* caffeine are responsible for what ails coffee drinkers. Caffeine, we have learned, produces one constellation of bodily abnormalities; the oils, acids and other compounds in coffee apparently produces another group of maladies.

For example, virtually all of the studies on coffee drinking accuse *caffeine* of being the major saboteur of the central nervous system (CNS). This is not at all surprising because of caffeine's long recognized and proven history as a CNS stimulant.

On the other hand, many of the studies on heart disease and cancer treat regular and decaffeinated coffees as equal enemies. Their findings suggest that the pathologies are dose-related but *not* caffeine-related. Thus, as a coffee drinker you are more prone to pancreatic and bladder cancer or heart diseases, as some studies indicate, and it makes little difference whether you're a regular or decaffeinated coffee drinker. If you drink *any* kind of coffee, you're increasing your risks of developing these diseases.

The same is true for much of the research on coffee consumption and gastrointestinal disturbances. They appear to be caused by coffee-produced variations in acid secretion and are not, we repeat, not necessarily related to *caffeine* consumption.

Thus, while the decaffeinated coffee producers make a big deal about relieving CNS symptoms such as sleeplessness or irritability, they obviously will not address themselves in television and radio commercials to the other coffee-related pathologies such as cancer, heart disease or gastrointestinal malfunctions.

The implication for coffee drinkers seems quite clear: the caffeine argument is at best, a half-issue. Coffee drinkers who value a healthy mind and body will quit drinking coffee *entirely*.

What Is Coffee?

Coffee is made from the roasted and ground beans of the coffee tree, and is *the* favorite hot drink in almost every country in temperate or cold climates.

The scientific name of the common coffee tree is Coffea arabica. It orginally grew wild in Ethiopia. It now is cultivated in Java, Sumatra, India, Arabia, Africa, Hawaii, Mexico, Central and South America, and the West Indies.[3]

The coffee grown in Brazil and Columbia equals more than the coffee grown by all other nations combined.[4]

Coffea arabica is a shrub with shiny, evergreen leaves. It is 14 to 20 feet high when fully grown, although coffee growers usually trim and prune the tree to 12 feet.

While there are more than 100 different kinds of coffee plants, the only two of importance here are Arabica and Robusta.

Together, they account for about 99 percent of world coffee production.

As the blossoms of the Coffea arabica turn a snowy white, the coffee berries gradually ripen from green to yellow to red, and that doesn't usually occur until the tree is at least five years old. The common variety grows best at altitudes from 2,000 to 6,000 feet.

The historical path of coffee from its origin in Ethiopia to the U.S. are a twisted voyage of fact and fiction.

In the beginning, coffee was variably used as a beverage, a food, a wine, and then a medicine. Coffee moved from Arabia to Turkey during the 1500s and to Italy in the 1600s. It hit European coffee houses in the 1600s and from there, the American colonies were not far behind.

Romantic and fanciful stories surround the discovery of the coffee bean and the tea leaf and the mysterious and wonderful things they could bring. In one such tale,[5] Kaldi, a legendary goatherd who lived in Abyssinia more than a thousand years ago, was startled to discover his flock prancing and cavorting all the sleepless night after eating some berries growing on a stand of short glossy green trees.

Kaldi, the legend continues, ate some of the berries himself and discovered what most of us know today: that coffee decreases drowsiness and fatigue, promotes mental alertness, enhances mental acuity and promotes rapid, clear thinking. At least, that's what is does for the short-term and when taken in small quantities. Taken in larger quantities and the prognosis is a great deal different.

The Dutch, credited by some historians with introducing tea to Europe also are credited with a fabulous legend.

According to this narrative,[6] a Chinese Buddhist had become quite tired during a nine-year meditation and had fallen asleep. When he ashamedly awoke, he was filled with guilt for his misdeed and proceeded to cut off his eyelids to guarantee an end to such sinful behavior.

His severed eyelids, the legend continues, landed on the ground and sprouted as the tea plant, which eventually provided the drink which we know is capable of banishing sleep.

Such are the legends of coffee and tea. But legend or not, the historical prospective of both tea and coffee is a record of the drug's ability to seriously affect the mind and body in ways which have universally, through all times and in all countries, been recognized as harmful.

The Danger From Tea

Tea drinkers face fewer health dangers compared to excessive coffee drinkers. And there are several reasons why this is true.

First, tea drinkers rarely drink their brew in the enormous quantities for which coffee drinkers are now famous. Most tea drinking is done at a level of a cup, or perhaps two, per day. A few tea drinkers in the U.S. may drink three or four cups a day. But never in our research, or that of any other studies we were able to find, did we encounter a tea drinker who regularly consumed 8, 10, or 15 cups of tea a day. Yet, millions of coffee drinkers put away 10 or 15 cups a day and think nothing of it.

Furthermore, caffeine levels in tea are substantially lower than that of most coffees. While it is possible to brew a cup of tea with 50 mg of caffeine, most teas contain about 35 mg per cup. Black teas average 40 mg per cup; green teas contain about 27 mg of caffeine per cup. A cup of coffee averages about 125 mg of caffeine.

It's readily apparent, then, that teas have much lower caffeine levels than either coffee or cola drinks, and therefore, tea is a great deal less harmful to your body, particularly your central nervous system.

Not only does tea contain less caffeine, it does not contain the same sorts of harmful oils and acids which *all* coffee contains, whether decaffeinated or not. And that's why the majority of research on tea and coffee exonerates tea from being linked to

Table 2. Comparison of brand and brewing time of mean caffeine content in tea.

type of tea	brewing time		
	2 min.	3 min.	5 min.
	mg. of caffeine/5 oz. cup		
Bagged tea			
black			
Brand A	33	46	50
Brand B	29	44	48
Brand C	21	35	39
Average mg, black bagged tea:	28	42	46
green			
Brand A	19	33	36
Brand B	9	20	26
Average mg, green bagged tea:	14	27	31
Oolong tea	13	30	40
Leaf tea			
Black, Brand A	31	38	40
Darjeeling	19	25	28
Oolong	17	20	24
Green	28	33	35
Japanese panfried	14	20	21
Japanese green	15	—	20
Average mg., leaf tea	21	27	28

Source: *Caffeine Content of Common Beverages,* Journal of the American Dietetic Association, January 1979.

many of the pathologies which haunt coffee drinkers. These include peptic ulcers, cancer of the bladder and pancreas, heart disease and gastrointestinal disorders.

Moreover, the caffeine content of teas has remained largely the same over history. Teas have not been subject to the insanity of mass market blending that has gone on so ruthlessly in the coffee business—particularly in the past 20 years. And it's that "special" blending that has caused so many of our caffeine troubles.

Coffee Dangers Are Increasing

It may be hard to believe, but as dangerous as coffee has always been, it's getting worse. And the blame for this growing danger can be directed at your friendly coffee producer and his economic bottom line.

Earlier, we mentioned the popularity of the coffee bean Coffea arabica. For centuries, this has been the most popular of all coffee beans in the U.S. and abroad, noted for its rich taste and hardy aroma. Other species of coffee beans were available, but they simply couldn't compare with the arabicas.

Enter: Coffea Robusta.

This hardy little bean, a product largely of Africa, India, Latin America and Indonesia, is changing all that. Robusta coffee was introduced in the early 1900s, but its decidedly unpleasant taste relegated it to a poor second choice among coffee producers.[7] But only for a while. More and more coffee producers became aware that what Robustas lacked in taste, they readily made up by something much more important: a richer, healthier net income.

The Robustas, in fact, make everybody happy—except the coffee consumer. The coffee growers love it because it is hardy, disease-resistance and it grows rapidly. As it can be grown at lower altitudes, it is not so susceptible to frost damage. And when a frost does occur, it fares better than Arabica. More importantly, it is easy to harvest and average yields are *more than double* the per-acre crop from Arabica.[8] Obviously, that's important to the producer, because they are readily available and—king of kings—*cheaper* than Arabicas.

Never mind that candid coffee experts have likened Robusta coffee's taste to that of burned rubber and its aroma to that of urine.[9] Robustas are *cheaper*.

And as you might expect, the use of Robustas in mass market coffees has been steadily increasing. The use of Arabicas has plummeted and are now the mainstay of gourmet coffee shops.

Statistics from the National Coffee Association show that U.S. imports of Robusta beans increased from 9.1 percent in 1959 to

31.9 in 1974. Present consumption remains high, although somewhat lower than 1974 levels.

More is Better

The significance of all this talk about Robusta is that these new wave beans have *twice* the amount of *caffeine* as Arabicas. And because Robustas are blended into nearly all U.S. mass market coffees, the dire effects caused by the coffee producers greed for fatter profit margins are readily apparent. You get stuck holding a grab bag of medical ills and bills, the full extent of which may take years to become manifest—and by then it may be too late.

But the public is getting the message about these Robustas. Even though they are largely unaware of this wholesale adulteration, *coffee consumption is declining*. Americans may not know exactly what the coffee producers are doing to their coffee, but they're casting their consumer votes against increased caffeine levels. They're voting *no* on coffee drinking.

What Is Caffeine?

Caffeine is an odorless, slightly bitter-tasting alkaloid chemical which is found naturally in several plants. It is widely distributed all over the world.

While it can be manufactured synthetically in the laboratory, most of the caffeine consumed in the U.S. is obtained from the seeds of Coffea arabica, robusta, Theobroma cacao, and from the leaves of Thea sinensis—the plants from which coffee, cocoa, and tea are made. The nuts of the tree Cola acuminata, from which various cola-flavored drinks are made, also contain about two percent caffeine.

Caffeine is chemically known as 1,3,7-trimethylxanthine, and belongs to a chemical family called methylated xanthines. It dissolves readily in water and alcohol and has crystals that look like little needles. Like cocaine, heroin and morphine, caffeine is white.

Table 3. Methylxanthine Contents of Foods and Drugs

Product	Caffeine (mgs)	Theobromine (mgs)	Theophylline (mgs)
Coffee (5 oz)			
Regular Brewed			
—percolated	110	3	tr
—dripolator	150	3.5	1
Instant	66	1.5	tr
Decaf Brewed	4.5	tr	tr
Instant Decaf	2	tr	tr
Soft Drinks (12 oz)			
Dr Pepper	61	tr	tr
Mr. Pibb	57	tr	tr
Mountain Dew	49	tr	tr
Tab	45	tr	tr
Coca-Cola	42	tr	tr
RC Cola	36	tr	tr
Pepsi-Cola	35	tr	tr
Diet Pepsi	34	tr	tr
Pepsi Light	34	tr	tr
Instant/Brewed Tea (5 min. brew)	45	9	6
Cocoa (5 oz)	13	173	tr
Milk Chocolate (1 oz)	6	42	tr
Drugs			
Vivarin Tablets	200	—	—
Nodoz	100	—	—
Excedrin	65	—	—
Vanquish	33	—	—
Empirin Compound	32	—	—
Anacin	32	—	—
Dristan	16.2	—	—

tr = less than 1 milligram per serving

Source: Reprinted from *Nutrition Action*, newsletter for Center for Science in the Public Interest.[13]

Other closely related compounds include theophylline (1,3-dimethyl xanthine) which is found in tea and theobromine (3,7-dimethyl xanthine) which is found in cocoa.

The xanthines found in these beverages differ greatly in their ability to affect your body. Caffeine, as you may well realize, is a most powerful stimulant to the CNS. Theobromine is the weakest of the three. And the xanthine found in chocolate and cocoa has no significant CNS effect.[10] [11]

The theophylline found in tea, however, has the greatest "shelf life" in your body. The body can metabolize the xanthine in tea at only about 15 percent per hour, whereas the half-life of caffeine is somewhat greater than 2-1/2 hours.

The metabolism of caffeine in the bodies of habitual users, however, has never been fully documented and some reports suggest that it may take days to decaffeinate the blood of habitual users.

Cocoa and chocolate differ markedly from tea and coffee in several ways. The latter are complete ciphers of nutritional benefit whereas cocoa and chocolate provide a high level of energy, along with significant amounts of calcium, iron, vitamin A and niacin. Thus, cocoa and chocolate provide the food energy for the stimulation they induce, while black coffee must *draw* on body reserves.[12]

Both coffee and caffeine have important medical implications, both short- and long-term. On a day-to-day basis, we'll show you how these chemicals disrupt the CNS, the cardiovascular and respiratory systems, and foul the gastrointestinal tract. Spreading our medical gaze to the near term, we can cite instances of chronic CNS disturbances, benign tumors, facial lesions, profound stomach disorders and other ailments. And lurking around a not-so-distant, long-term corner may be cancer, heart disease, ulcers, birth defects, breast cancer, and other crippling and fatal pathologies.

In all likelihood, you're already too familiar with some of these annoying and painful conditions from your own coffee drinking past. You've had that drugged up "hyper" feeling. You've had the stomach pains and nausea. Maybe you've even had heart problems, ulcers or breast tumors.

Well, if you keep up your habit, it's quite possible—even likely—that the distressing symptoms you now have will *intensify*. With increased drug use, you may develop newer, more dangerous diseases. Such is the prognosis for the users of this hazardous, addictive drug.

Coffee, we owe it all to you.

3

Coffee:
The All-American Elixir

There probably is no beverage on the face of the earth as pervasive as coffee. There undoubtedly is no drug as prevalent in the food and drink of Americans as caffeine. Taken together, 1,3,7-trimethylxanthine is an almost inescapable poison which taints our systems from birth—even before birth—until death.

In 1976, 101 million people 20 years of age and over in the U.S. drank coffee. At the time, that was 80 pecent of the civilian, noninstitutionalized population.[1] Non-coffee drinkers were about as popular as teetotalers at a college beer bust.

The average amount consumed by coffee drinkers was 3.2 cups per day, which is an average of 2.6 cups per day for *all* Americans 20 years of age and older.[2]

The U.S. Is The Champ

Today, Americans gulp down some 380 million cups of coffee at the rate of 2.02 cups per person.[3] Each U.S. citizen drinks the brew of about 12 pounds of coffee each year, and obviously, many of them drink a great deal more.

Each year, the United States uses 2,600,000,000 pounds of coffee, or about one-third of all the coffee grown in the world. While the Swedes and Finns drink more coffee per capita ("lucky" for them), the good 'ol U.S. of A. far outstrips the Swedes in coffee imported and total coffee drank.

Tea consumption in America is only one-quarter that of coffee, but this still constitutes more than forty billion tea servings a year, and enough caffeine, in all likelihood, to kill all the rats in all the laboratories on the face of the earth.

Caffeine—The Addictive Additive

Added to the coffee addiction is the rapidly growing dependency on soft drinks containing caffeine. It's not bad enough that caffeine occurs *naturally* in coffee and tea, but U.S. manufacturers *add caffeine* to soft drinks whether we like it or not.

In fact, the government *requires* that caffeine be included in cola and pepper drinks and *permits* it to be added to other soft drinks. Under current standards, the presence of caffeine, rather than cola nut extract, is the mark of a true "cola."[4] All this occurs while the FDA admits that it does not know, for sure, how many deleterious effects this drug causes.

And where do you suppose all that caffeine in those soft drinks comes from? Why, from coffee, of course.

Caffeine is removed from coffee through one of several processes, the most widely used involving harsh solvents which separate caffeine from the coffee beans.

The bulk caffeine is removed, refined and then added to a wide variety of soft drinks, foods and medicines. Most of the caffeine is used to spike soft drinks, those cans of soft drinks that children and young adults swill down by the billions each day.

According to the FDA, caffeine used in soft drinks accounts for perhaps up to 90 percent of a total dietary use of added caffeine.[5]

And check this, more than 2,000,000 pounds of caffeine are annually purged from coffee, caffeine which is used to adulterate your foods and medicines.

Caffeine is added to certain over-the-counter drugs, including headache, allergy, cold and stay-awake remedies and in foods such as baked goods, frozen dairy products, soft candy, gelatins and puddings, mostly as flavoring.

In short, caffeine is everywhere, whether you like it or not. It's in the coffee and tea you drink. It's in soft drinks which cool your throat but poison your mind and stomach. It's in the foods you eat and the medicines you take.

We serve these products in our homes, schools and churches. It's found in our restaurants, our hospitals and in our mental institutions. Psychiatric patients, children and seniors in retirement homes are regularly fed mind-bending doses of caffeine.

Thus, its influence is virtually inescapable. And for millions of people, certainly for at least 15,000,000 coffee addicts, the total intake of caffeine from these sources can truly be mind boggling. Never have Americans been so exposed to this debilitating drug. Never has it been more important to rid our systems of this noxious, poisonous chemical.

Coffee Drinking Is On The Way Out

Coffee drinking in the U.S. has been slipping almost continuously for the past 30 years—an economic maelstrom that the $7 billion coffee industry has been helpless to curtail.

And it's readily apparent that Americans are becoming unhappy with what coffee is doing to their minds and bodies and they are seeking other beverages—although not always safer ones—as substitutes. Perhaps as I suggested, Americans are getting fed up with the higher caffeine levels in the new wave of Robusta blend coffees that are being produced.

In 1950, for example, more than three-fourths of the U.S. population over the age of 10 was drinking coffee at a rate of 2.38 cups per person.

Table 4. Percentage of the Population Drinking Coffee

	1962	1977	1979	1980	Change 62-80	Change 79-80
10-19	25.1	12.8	7.2	7.9	-17.2	+0.7
20-29	81.0	48.6	45.6	45.1	-35.9	-0.5
30-59	90.8	77.3	78.0	75.3	-15.5	-2.7
60+	88.4	82.5	81.3	81.7	-6.7	+0.4

Source: Reprinted from summary of National Coffee Drinking Survey Winter 1980, Data Group, Inc., Elkins Park, Pa, National Coffee Association of the U.S.A., Inc.

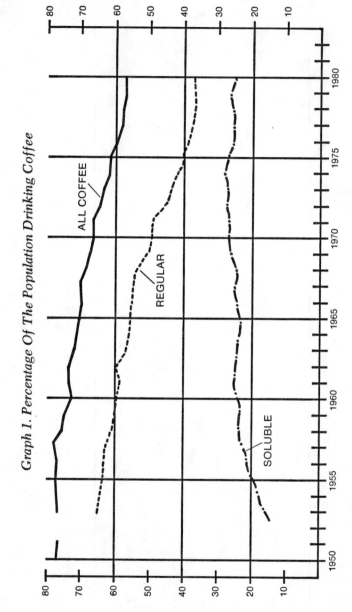

Graph 1. Percentage Of The Population Drinking Coffee

ALL COFFEE

REGULAR

SOLUBLE

Source: Reprinted from summary of National Coffee Drinking Survey Winter 1980, Data Group, Inc., Elkins Park, Pa. National Coffee Association of the U.S.A., Inc.

In its most recent survey, the London-based National Coffee Association (NCA) reported that coffee drinking during the 1980 winter slipped to 2.06 cups per day. Only 57.2 percent of the over 10 group according to the NCA, was drinking the brew.

The Coffee Association surveys are taken every year in winter when the cold weather swells coffee drinking statistics to their highest seasonal levels.

Typically, coffee consumption increases during the early adult years as people start to drink coffee regularly.[6] Once they have started, they increase the number of cups they drink daily, sometimes to exorbitant levels. Coffee drinkers who polish off 30 and even 40 cups a day are not uncommon. And there are a great many people, millions in fact, who regularly drink anywhere from 5-15 cups per day.

In later years, people begin to cut down their coffee drinking but they do not, ordinarily, give it up completely. Millions of people in the over-50 age group drink only one cup of coffee per day.

Younger and Smarter?

In recent years, however, young people are taking a different tact and coffee drinking statistics are changing accordingly.

Studies by the National Coffee Association show that persons under 30 years of age are drinking considerably less coffee than in previous years and considerably less coffee than those *over* thirty.

While that news is gratifying, however, the picture is not an entirely rosy one. It's this younger age group that is drinking a disproportionately larger share of soft drinks that contain caffeine—the same caffeine they would have been drinking had they been drinking coffee.

In other words, *coffee* drinking among the 30 and under set may have declined, but their total *caffeine* consumption may be reaching all-time highs. And as a result, the caffeine consumers themselves may be reaching all-time highs as well.

Graph 2. Index of Coffee Drinkers Under and Over 30 Years of Age.

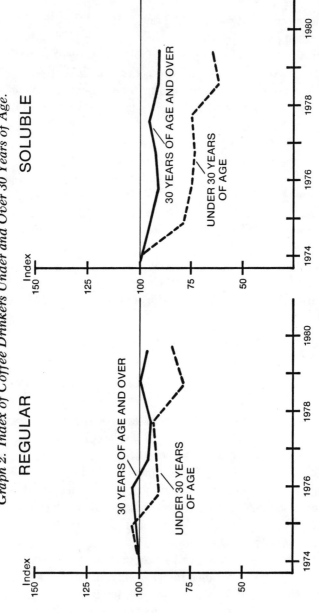

Source: Reprinted from summary of National Coffee Drinking Survey Winter 1980, Data Group, Inc., Elkins Park, Pa., National Coffee Association of the U.S.A., Inc.

In percentages, nearly 36 percent fewer people between the ages of 20 and 29 are drinking coffee. The figures, prepared by the NCA can also be plotted graphically, where the result is even more dramatic.

The Likely Coffee Addicts

In a study by what was the U.S. Department of Health, Education and Welfare, a profile has been established which sheds light on those who are more likely to become coffee addicts.

The study, completed in 1976, shows that heavy coffee drinkers differ from those who drink little or no coffee in several significant ways.

In general, men were more likely than women to report drinking coffee and men were also more likely to report drinking more than five cups of coffee per day.

White persons are more likely to be heavy drinkers than either black persons or persons of other races.

Heavy coffee drinking was found to be related to family income, with heavy coffee drinkers also likely to have higher incomes. That result, however, may also be linked with age, with middle-aged persons more likely to be earning higher salaries.

In general, persons with the most and persons with the least education were *less* likely to drink five or more cups per day, than those with a medium amount of education.

Two occupational groups, manager-administrators and craftsmen, tended to have higher percentages of heavy coffee drinkers than other occupational groups.

One more note on coffee drinkers: drug users tend to be drug users. That is, people who are heavy coffee drinkers tend to get involved with other sorts of drugs, cigarettes, alcohol, etc. Obviously, the synergistic effect of such combinations can create multiple effects.

For example, one study shows that smokers are nearly *four times* as likely to be heavy coffee drinkers as those who have

Table 5. How cigarette smoking influences coffee consumption.
Daily coffee drinking levels go up as cigarette smoking goes up.

Cigarette smoking status	Number of persons in thousands	Daily coffee consumption		
		Total	5 or more cups	Less than 5 cups
Never smoked	54,078	100.0	8.3	91.7
Former smoker	25,852	100.0	17.3	82.7
Present smoker	45,740	100.0	29.6	70.4
			Percent in distribution	
Total	126,429	100.0	17.9	82.1

Source: Reprinted from DHEW Publication No. (PHS) 80-1559.

never smoked and nearly twice as likely to be heavy coffee drinkers as those who *used* to smoke cigarettes.

And speaking of the behavior of heavy coffee drinkers, it's interesting to note that as coffee consumption levels *increase*, use of decaffeinated coffee *decreases*.

In one government study, it was found that whereas 70 percent of the one cup-per-day drinkers use regular coffee, almost 82 percent of the drinkers who consume six cups a day use regular. Conversely, about 11 percent of the heavy coffee drinkers use decaffeinated coffee, but the number more than doubles to 23 percent among one cup-per-day drinkers.

Decaffeinated Coffee Use Is Rising

For years, decaffeinated coffee consumption was so insignificant a part of the total coffee picture that the National Coffee Association didn't even catalog consumption levels until 1958.

In that year, the report showed that Americans drank an average of .04 cups a day per person. It was up to .15 in 1970. In the most recent year, consumption reached .034 cups per person, or 2.58 cups per decaffeinated coffee drinker. The association also reported that at least 13 percent of the population drinks decaffeinated coffee. That's about a two and one-half percent increase since 1977.

Breakfast of Champions

Coffee is losing its hold as the number one breakfast drink. For years, it reigned supreme as *the* breakfast drink for most adults and older children, but between 1962 and 1980, a drop of about one-quarter cup per person, per-day was noted.

Far more important is the finding that coffee is losing much more ground as a beverage at meals *other than* breakfast, where coffee showed a decrease of more than 50 percent, from .98 cups to .41 cups in 1980.

Picking up the slack in these statistics are fruit and vegetable juices which, together with soft drinks, became the leading gainers when compared to coffee, tea and hot cocoa or chocolate. And the figures held up throughout the day.

The Bottom Line

The relevance of all this is that coffee is dropping out as the number 1 beverage in the U.S. Americans are discovering in ever-increasing numbers, that coffee is the bum drink of the 80s. Through self-discovery, they are learning that not only does coffee produce zero nutritional benefits, it can lead to pain and discomforts both large and small, and may, in fact, lead to pathologies that are far worse.

They need no doctors to discover this. In truth, the medical community is probably providing a great disservice to the patient community by its silence on the coffee issue, and worse, by its misinformation about the controversy.

The conclusion to be drawn from all this is that coffee, truly the omnipresent drug of the 60s and 70s, is on the way out. Whereas nearly 80 percent of the population used to drink coffee, only about 56 percent now indulge in this dangerous habit. The inescapable truth to be drawn from these dwindling numbers is that Americans are getting wise to what coffee has been doing to them, and they don't want any part of it, decaffeinated or otherwise. And they're not alone.

More and more research is pointing an accusing finger at the role of caffeine and coffee in the development of a growing number of ailments and diseases. Newspaper and magazine articles by the hundreds and thousands are adding their weight and credibility against these destructive substances. Coffee victims *themselves* are conducting their own informal research and are kicking the habit in record numbers. Their chronicles of self-research are made all the more impressive because their self-prescriptions *worked*. Let the doctors, clinicians, and researchers haggle over the fine points of medical research; these patients *know* what is causing their problems. They *know* that coffee is dangerous to their health, and yours.

4

How We Get Hooked

There have been a great number of books written about why people take drugs, but remarkably few have undertaken the question of why people abuse coffee and caffeine.

Medical authorities point to the fact that using drugs to alter consciousness is nothing new—it's been going on for thousands of years. And in this respect, coffee's ability to reduce lethargy, to stimulate and enliven, are legendary. There is no need here to chronicle coffee's historical spread across the world.

In fact the only thing new about drug use is the fact that the user's preferences have been undergoing important changes. Younger Americans are coming to prefer marijuana and a variety of hallucinogenic drugs rather than alcohol. Older Americans have stuck with booze, coffee, and certain types of stimulant drugs.

But what happens to make a coffee drinker of the cup or two-per-day magnitude into the addictive user who drinks 5, 10, 15 or more cups per day?

Here, science is virtually mute.

In our study, we learned that all coffee drinkers *started* their addictive careers with a cup or two per day. Everybody starts that way. Alcoholics began with just one drink. Smokers took just one puff.

It was equally obvious from our study that these novice coffee drinkers *must have liked* the effect coffee gave them, although different folks get different strokes.

Coffee's Rewards

Some respondents in our survey said they enjoyed the *taste* of coffee, and this agreeable taste was what kept them coming back for more. Others talked about the great "pick me up" coffee gave them, how it aroused their sleepy brains and got them into action for their working (or recreational) day.

At work, their mental acuity and alertness was heightened with more coffee. It was part of the coffee break ritual, the great social lubricant of the workplace.

Obviously, all this is very agreeable. So why did they decide to quit? Simple, the disadvantages of coffee drinking began to outweigh the advantages.

Thus, on the one hand, we have a situation where people begin coffee drinking because they enjoy its rewards. At the other end of the coffee drinking continuum, we have the "quitters" who became fed up with coffee's harmful effects. But in between, we have a scientific puzzle. Why do coffee drinkers escalate from the lower, *enjoyable* levels of coffee use to the higher, unenjoyable levels? What causes them to slide into addictive use?

Coffee Use Over Time

According to one study on the subject, coffee drinkers begin their careers at low levels. In the early stages, however, the mold is usually cast. Whereas a cup or two is the order of the day for many

Graph 3. Percent of persons 20 years of age and over by daily coffee consumption and age.

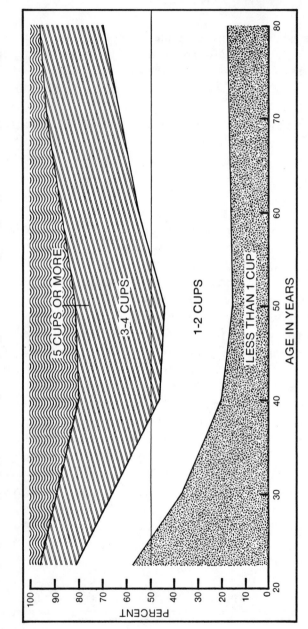

Source: National Center for Health Statistics. U.S. Department of Health, Education, Welfare.

coffee drinking beginners, it is not for others. Their daily consumption slowly, inexonerably, creeps upward—all without apparent notice.

Thus, 17 percent of the coffee drinking population begins drinking three cups of coffee each day; 11 percent creeps up to four cups a day; 7 percent reaches five cups a day; and a whopping 16 percent is gulping down six or more cups a day.[1]

It's obvious, then, that *moderation* is the exception, rather than the rule. *In fact, more than half of the U.S. adult coffee drinking population consumes coffee in amounts which nearly all medical authorities agree is harmful to their health.*

What Coffee Drinkers Say

Most of the respondents in our research told us they began their coffee drinking innocently enough and that their consumption crept upward "for no apparent reason."

"I just suddenly noticed one day," said a 30-year-old secretary, "that I was drinking an awful lot of coffee. And I'm not really sure how it got that high."

That sort of reaction typifies what we heard. And in most instances, the addictive consumption levels didn't become apparent until some physical or mental aberration decisively brought it to their attention.

The Addictive Hooks: Tolerance And Withdrawal

In an earlier chapter, I discussed the role of tolerance as being one of the principal progenitors of addiction. Tolerance is the simple notion that over time, it takes a larger and larger dose of a drug to obtain the effect that smaller doses used to produce. It is precisely the reason why smokers light up 20 or 30 times a day instead of five or ten; the very same reason why alcoholics consume great quantities of their booze: small quantities just aren't as "good" anymore.

That's why coffee drinkers put away 5, 10, 15 up to 40 and 50 cups per day. To get the desired effect, they *have to* drink larger and larger quantities.

Thus, we have the *carrot*, the desired effect we want coffee to produce. We also have the stick. If coffee drinkers *don't* get their fix of coffee, painful withdrawal symptoms will often begin.

One group of researchers has shown that abstinence from coffee increases anxiety and muscle tension, whereas coffee consumption will decrease these symptoms. Therefore, the habit is *continued* because of a daily need to eliminate the anxiety, the headaches, the tension, and the other withdrawal effects caused by coffee abstinence.

In all likelihood, these two addictive elements—tolerance and withdrawal—are why we have millions and millions of coffee addicts today. New tolerance levels push them to larger and larger coffee doses; withdrawal sends them back to the coffeepot everyday to relieve their painful symptoms. And it is truly a dilemma which can and must be broken. For the pain, suffering and disease this addiction begets is truly epidemic in proportion.

5

Coffee And The CNS

Paula S. is a 26-year-old administrative assistant for a Chicago insurance company who picked up her coffee drinking habit from her mother, who in turn, probably picked it up from hers.

She averaged 12 cups of coffee per day which she drank at an office, where her fellow employees drank "pot after pot after pot." Her job was fraught with pressure, a condition which her coffee drinking most assuredly worsened.

She reported being constantly jittery, all hyped up. In fact, she likened her behavior to being doped up on "speed," a drug she had experimented with and dropped because she didn't like its effects.

Paula suffered at times from a faulty memory and impaired mental abilities. At times, she said, she just couldn't think straight. "It was just like I was moving real fast. I just can't describe it."

Fortunately for Paula, she kicked the habit, and only then did she become fully aware of how damaging coffee had been to her central nervous system.

"That funny buzzing in my head has disappeared, and I can finally think straight—it's the first time I've been able to do that in years. In fact, this is the first time I've been able to recognize my *real* self from my false self. Believe me, it's a welcome change."

●

Nobody knows how people of the U.S. would behave if they were free from the caffeine drug habit.

Think about that a minute.

How would we even *function* without our morning cup of coffee? What would happen to productivity levels if employees were not always feeding their habit (on the job, no less) and bringing their drug-related hangups to the factories and offices of the land? How many business deals are lost and otherwise screwed up because of the mind-bending effects of coffee? How would a clear-headed populace behave?

The question was posed by one of our interviewees who had kicked the caffeine habit and noticed, to her amazement, that her well-being improved in ways she never thought possible. Her powers of concentration were vastly improved. She was calm, collected, "on the ball" as it were. She got along well with her supervisors and co-workers. She noticed the changes. Her co-workers noticed them as well. And she wondered aloud during our interview, how much better the country's productivity would be if the coffee addicts of the world kicked their habits. I wonder too.

Coffee And Productivity

There have been no studies of which I am aware that have grappled with the question of whether caffeine or coffee impairs productivity or work habits. It could easily be suggested, however, that workers who suffer from caffeinism also turn in inferior work performances. Headaches, jitteriness, irritability, difficulties in concentration, mood swings and the whole constellation of caffeine overdose symptoms can certainly drain productivity from business and industry. Health and behavioral changes caused by the coffee addict do not occur in a vacuum. And workers who suffer from its effects suffer them *on the job* as well as off the job. It's a simple fact: employees who don't feel well don't perform well.

Perhaps the closest study that parallels on-the-job productivity was one recently conducted at the University of Oklahoma where a psychologist has come up with some surprising findings about the relationship between caffeine consumption and college grades.

Researchers Dr. Kirby Gilliland and Dara Andress, a graduate student in psychology, ran the research project in which both men and women students were grouped in four caffeine consumption groups.

The differences in academic performances, according to Gilliland, were striking.

The abstainers and low consumers of coffee had grade point averages of C-pluses. The moderate and high consumers of coffee had averages of C-minuses.

Gilliland claims the study shows a strong negative relationship between caffeine consumption and success in academic performance.

Gilliland also reported the high-caffeine consumers thought they suffered more deleterious effects from their caffeine intake than did any other group. They reported more psychophysiological disorders including digestive problems such as heartburn and diarrhea.

Whether or not these results could be applied in any wholesale way to the performance of workers in business and industry, however, is quite another matter.

In academia, Gilliland says his study means that the more caffeine you consume, the more likely you are to do less well, become more depressed, more anxious and have psychophysiological symptoms. In the workaday marketplace, where success is so highly prized and coffee drinking habits so much more ingrained, I would expect the same results—perhaps even more so.

It will become altogether obvious in this chapter that caffeine can and does product remarkable changes in the central nervous system—changes that will bode ill-tidings for the coffee drinker—and his *employer.*

Facts in Fantasyland

Anyone who's ever seen Robert Young in the TV commercials knows that caffeine is responsible for toxic effects in humans that result in symptoms of central nervous system poisoning such as nervousness and irritability. The characters central to Young's commercials are always people who are strung out on coffee: jumpy, cross, short-tempered, the whole lot. These people are obviously coffee addicts. They are drinking excessive amounts of coffee and their moody behavior is shown, quite rightly, as having a dire effect on their jobs and personal relationships. They are suffering from the toxic effects of coffee. But it's clear from the commercial that they have not been willing to do anything about the cause-effect relationship. They are obviously hooked. Worse yet, they don't know it.

Decaffeinated coffee is the answer, says Young, and sure enough, these willy-nillies kick the caffeine habit and begin to behave like docile children at Sunday prayer breakfast.

The Truth About Caffeine And Your CNS

It is news to no one that coffee can make you behave like the nervous nellies in a Robert Young coffee commercial. Coffee has been doing this to people and goats since Kaldi got his first fix in an Abyssinian pasture thousands of years ago. We've known about the coffee's adverse effects all along—but it has only been in recent years that the pendulum has begun to swing the other way *against* coffee, and particularly against coffee containing caffeine.

Why the sudden switch? Why are Americans moving away from coffee in numbers that are beginning to panic the coffee producers of the world?

Americans are getting wise, that's why. We're getting more serious about our nutrition, about our physical health, about the vast number of chemicals which are polluting our lands, our rivers and lakes, and our bodies.

We want to *live*. We're beginning to understand that good health means good nutrition and a clean environment. We're beginning to learn that life's pleasures don't have to include addictions to endless varieties of damaging drugs: nicotine, alcohol, coffee, narcotics. We can and will kick these habits.

Getting High On Caffeine

When you take a swig of coffee, it rolls down through your gastrointestinal tract where it is easily absorbed by your body. It reaches a peak plasma level in about one hour and passes quickly into the central nervous system.[1]

Once in the CNS, caffeine's first target is the cortex and the medulla. It also stimulates the medullary respiratory, vasomotor and vagal centers. These are the systems which are responsible for such important functions as breathing, blood vessel dilation and operation of the vagus nerve which provides innervation to the larynx, lungs, heart, esophagus and most of the abdominal organs.

How dramatically these nerve centers are affected depends largely on the dose of caffeine. Drink a little, and the effect is minimal. Drink a lot and you could be in serious trouble, and perhaps even die.

Caffeine Overdose

A lethal dose of caffeine for a healthy, adult male is about 10 grams. That's about 70, eight-ounce cups of the strongest coffee you're ever likely to drink. There has never been a reported case of a fatality from drinking too much coffee. The reasons why this is so are twofold. First, coffee is very quickly metabolized and excreted, and therefore it's almost impossible to accumulate a lethal dose in our systems. Secondly, drinking that much coffee is likely to cause extreme vomiting, and this again will reduce caffeine accumulations. But all of this is not to say that people have not been killed by caffeine overdose. Because they have, both by cardiac arrest and respiratory failure.

Lethal Caffeine Poisoning

One of the first such cases reported in recent history was in 1959 when a 35-year-old woman was accidentally administered 3.2 grams of caffeine in a solution intravenously. The patient began convulsing, stopped breathing and died. Still another hospital patient was given 0.4 grams of caffeine in the same solution and experienced convulsions. Fortunately for this patient, the error was discovered in time, the caffeine solution immediately halted, and the patient recovered.[2]

And there are other records of caffeine overdose. A five-year-old girl ate handfuls of Tri-Aqua tablets one Sunday evening, apparently thinking they were candy. Tri-Aqua is a diuretic and contains about 99 mg of caffeine per tablet.

Within an hour, the little girl complained to her mother of "cold chills" and stomach cramps. Her condition steadily worsened and within four hours she was pronounced dead on arrival at a local hospital. Her caffeine intake had exceeded 5 grams. She had consumed 54 tablets.[3]

A 45-year-old woman was given 50 grams of caffeine instead of 50 grams of glucose during a routine test. A few minutes later she began to vomit. She died about two hours later. Her caffeine intake had been enough to kill *five* healthy men.[4]

But, not all of the caffeine deaths have been accidental. Caffeine also provides the mentally disturbed with a method to commit suicide. One case involved a 27-year-old woman who was found dead in bed with a suicide note. Her death was ascribed to an overdose of caffeine. The vehicle was apparently an over-the-counter drug.[5]

Common Caffeine Maladies

Thus, caffeine has a demonstrated capability of killing people. There are no ifs, ands or buts about it. Caffeine can kill.

Taken in small doses, however, the effects are still toxic.

Of all the reasons for dumping the coffee habit, none seems so compelling as the need to escape the havoc that caffeine drinking brings to your mind. By far and away, that's why most people decide to kick the habit.

Pharmacologists consider daily doses of caffeine which exceed 250 mg as "large."[6] Between 15,000,000 and 30,000,000 people drink anywhere from 700 mg or better. You can certainly realize then, the potential for great abuse of this chemical.

The symptoms of central nervous system disorders have now been fairly well categorized. They include mood disturbances, sleep disruptions and withdrawal symptoms (a subject we dealt with more fully in Chapter 12).

The most common anxiety manifestations of caffeinism are frequent urination, jitteriness, tremulousness, agitation, irritability, muscle twitchings, lightheadedness, rapid breathing, rapid heart beat, and cardiac palpitations.[7]

Obviously, not everyone experiences all of these symptoms and not all people experience these symptoms in the same degree.

Our research group voiced much the same litany of complaints. Jitteriness, agitation and irritability led the way of commonly mentioned symptoms.

The secretary of a large Midwestern restaurant chain told us she quit drinking coffee just to find out how much of her energy was naturally her own—and how much was created by her coffee consumption.

"I found out that at least *half* my energy was from caffeine," she noted. "And here I thought I had such a dynamic personality. It was the coffee!"

She went on to report that she believed her caffeine use allowed her to physically overextend. Had she listened to her body, it would have told her to slow down. But the caffeine disguised the "go slow" cues and she found she was making a wreck of herself. "I was constantly worn out," she said.

The woman's observation correlates perfectly with a recent study which showed that caffeine inhibits a natural mechanism that tries to tell your body to slow down.

A research team led by Dr. Solomon Snyder, director of neuroscience at Johns Hopkins University School of Medicine, pinpointed the method by which caffeine acts as a stimulant. Snyder said the discovery may point the way to improved drugs. Snyder and his group of researchers theorize that caffeine might work by blocking the action of a compound called adenosine, which they already were investigating.

Adenosine is one of the building blocks of DNA, and is involved in cellular energy. But its crucial function, as far as Snyder is concerned, is its role as a "neuromodulator" that tends to depress activity.

The researchers also studied close relatives of caffeine, including theophylline, and showed that the stimulant effect of each was proportional to its ability to block the natural anti-activity chemical, Snyder said.

Caffeine And Your Sleep

One of the most common complaints among coffee drinkers is that the caffeine can disturb their sleep. Such results have been known for thousands of years, and in fact, is one of the reasons why many drink coffee in the first place: to stay awake.

Some coffee drinkers, on the other hand, claim that their sleep is as restful as ever, regardless of their coffee consumption. And without statistical evidence, who can refute their testimony.

While it is obvious that caffeine affects all of us in different ways, it is equally interesting to note that we oftentimes *don't know* how coffee is affecting our system, and therefore, we cannot evaluate what's happening to our sleep.

Many of the respondents in our research reported findings which parallel the formal research on the subject: coffee drinkers don't have the least idea what a good night's sleep is all about—so rarely have they recently had one.

In brain wave studies,[8] researchers have found that caffeine impairs the quality of sleep during the first three hours, a fact which agrees with the metabolic elimination of caffeine by the liver.

Another researcher noted that caffeine consumption not only substantially delays the onset of sleep, but diminishes the quality of sleep as well. Significantly more body movements were noted among high caffeine users and the quality of sleep was substantially diminished.[9]

Coffee Drinkers
Are The Last To Know

One study proved just how ignorant we may be about our sleep. The researcher studied the sleeping habits of medical students and found that many students *claimed* caffeine did not disturb their sleep, even when objective observations confirmed that it had. This denial, says the researcher, reinforces the clinical impression that many coffee drinkers simply don't attribute undesirable clinical symptoms to their caffeine intake.[10]

This situation illuminates one of the insidious aspects of coffee addiction: we often are unaware of how it effects us. Time after time in our study, respondents reported improved energy levels produced by better, more restful sleep.

What is more remarkable is that they believed they *had* been getting a good night's sleep. In short, coffee is ruining the sleep of millions of Americans—and they don't even know it.

Coffee's Secret CNS Punishment

Coffee not only is secretly ruining the sleep of millions of addicts, it is intruding on their lives and their health, in many other stealthy ways.

"I didn't realized how lousy it was making me feel until I quit," a 37-year-old housewife told us. "I just can't believe it was doing such a heavy number on me."

Comments like these really formed a consensus in our research. A woman who drank coffee for 25 years reported that coffee made her jittery—a fact she didn't recognize until she kicked the habit.

"I know for me, when I'm not drinking coffee, I have more energy," said a 37-year-old saleswoman. "I sleep better. I wake up in the morning feeling better and I'm not as nervous."

Another candid respondent told us he would frequently become depressed on weekends and couldn't figure out what was wrong. After he had quit, his depression disappeared. It was caused, he said, by his *lack* of coffee on weekends.

A young secretary who drank up to eight cups of coffee a day told us how everyone remarked "how much calmer I was" after she had quit drinking coffee.

Another eight-cups-a-day drinker, this one 25 years old, told us she "certainly didn't know (coffee drinking) was causing that much change in my personality."

A 42-year-old executive told us his six to eight cups a day habit of 20 years was far more damaging than he would have admitted—before he quit. "I found that coffee has much more of a lingering effect than I thought it had. Now that I've quit, I'm almost evangelical about it. I realize that coffee had probably been bothering me a lot longer than I had realized."

Again and again, we were told of these tales of significant CNS disturbances—upheavals which the victims were *totally unaware.* It was only after they had quit the drug that they realized the gravity of their addiction, and the degree of their physiological disturbances.

CNS Overdose

The most critical danger of coffee addiction is the CNS overdose which brings some patients to the brink of mental disaster—a frightening emergency which neither they, nor oftentimes their doctors, are prepared to meet.

Take the case of a group of patients at Walter Reed Army Medical Center in Washington, D.C., reported by Dr. John F. Greden, M.D., director of psychiatric research.[11] In a paper published by Greden, he relates the case of a 27-year-old nurse who applied for an evaluation at the outpatient clinic because of lightheadedness, tremulousness, breathlessness, headache, and irregular heartbeat which occurred sporadically two or three times a day.

The symptoms, according to Greden, had developed gradually over a three-week period. She denied precipitating stresses. When the evaluating physician commented on her apparent anxiety, she admitted being apprehensive, but correlated it with the presence of the palpitations, chest discomfort and irregular heartbeat.

The woman thereafter underwent a battery of laboratory tests, a physical exam and an electrocardiogram. The tests revealed nothing unusual, save premature ventricular contractions, a characteristic feature of anxiety reactions.

During her final session with the evaluating internist, the woman was given drugs for her heart problem and then referred to the psychiatric outpatient clinic for treatment for what the internist said was "anxiety reaction (probably secondary to the fear that her husband would be transferred to Viet Nam)."

But the woman was unmoved by the doctor's analysis. So, like more than 90 percent of the respondents of our survey, she came up with her own self-diagnosis: she reasoned her problems were due to her excessive coffee consumption.

Thus, she decided to kick the coffee habit and within 36 hours, virtually all symptoms disappeared, including her cardiovascular arrhythmias. She complained of fatigue for one week, but then began noticing, like many others in our study, that she was "truly awake in the morning for the first time in years."

Later, she "challenged" her system by temporarily returning to her coffee habit. Immediately, the heart problems returned, documented by another EKG. A two-year follow-up revealed that her symptoms have never recurred.

●

Greden goes on to relate other cases in which doctors failed to identify the symptoms produced by excessive coffee consumption, and instead, mistakenly blamed the symptoms on anxiety neurosis.

A 37-year-old Army lieutenant colonel was referred from the medical clinic to a psychiatric outpatient facility because of a *two-year history* of "chronic anxiety." After three complete medical workups (all negative), and months of taking prescribed medications to ease the condition, a psychiatrist finally delved into his caffeine consumption and learned the lieutenant was drinking between 8 and 14 cups of coffee per day.

The psychiatrist's prescription for the lieutenant was easy: Kick the coffee habit. He did. And that was the end of his problems.

●

Still another similar case was that of a 34-year-old Army personnel sergeant who underwent three medical exams and batteries of tests, both medical and psychological. Only after these expensive, time-consuming tests were completed, however, did anyone think to ask him about his caffeine use. When it was found that he was drinking between 10 and 15 cups a day, the prescription was the simple *elimination* of one of his drugs—not the *addition* of others. He kicked the caffeine habit and his problems disappeared.

Other cases have been revealed in which doctors mistakenly identified the symptoms produced by excessive coffee consumption as anxiety neurosis. In our own research, the results were much the same, only worse. Doctors consistently failed to take adequate medical histories which would have warned them of the patient's excessive coffee consumption. Had they done so, they would have been better equipped to evaluate whether the patient's complaint was caused by caffeine overdose, or some other condition.

These findings are supported by a study in Belfast, Northern Ireland.

Here, the 28-year-old patient of a consulting psychiatrist reported that she suddenly developed palpitations and panic one evening, followed by persistent anxiety attacks of cold sweat, shortness of breath, and at times, tingling of the extremities.

A comprehensive psychiatric examination convinced the doctor to look elsewhere for her problem. Being aware of earlier studies, he inquired into her coffee consumption. After learning she was drinking 20 cups of strong coffee each day, the doctor prescribed completely quitting coffee. She did and 10 days later her panic had disappeared. Three weeks later she was without symptoms and all drug prescriptions were stopped.

The doctor's concluding remarks have a universal application for doctors around the world. "At the present time," he said, "it is quite likely that some patients are receiving anxiolytic (tranquilizing) drugs which are not only useless for this (anxiety) condition, but may unnecessarily prolong a curable condition." The doctor, he concluded, "can learn of its existence by simply asking a few questions."[12]

•

In another case report,[13] a 28-year-old Alaskan fisherman who was competing in a 1,049-mile dog sled race virtually blew his mind with a caffeine overdose—but recovered.

The Iditarod Trail International Sled Dog Race is held annually between Anchorage and Nome, to commemorate a route used decades ago by runners bringing diphtheria serum to Nome.

In the third week of the competition, the strapping fisherman, a veteran of two previous races, decided to mush continuously for 48 hours. Following an evening meal of pork chops, two cups of brewed coffee, and three cola drinks, he resumed mushing. Despite his caffeine intake, estimated at 270 and 330 mg, he ingested 400 mg of Vivarin, an over-the-counter, stay-awake preparation. Twenty minutes later, he ingested 400 mg more— making a total of 1,000 mg of caffeine in less than three hours.

Half an hour later, trouble began. His hands became tremulous and he experienced a pronounced buzzing in his ears. He perceived his miner's headlamp as emitting no more than a narrow band of light. He described the ascent of a long hill as "if it were a flat plain riddled with white stars."

Soon, vertigo struck the fisherman and twice he fell from his sled. When morning came, some six hours later, the symptoms had slowly subsided and he completed the race. Doctors examined him and, noting his symptoms of impaired memory, altered levels of consciousness, visual illusions and hallucinations, described his condition as caffeine-induced delirium.

•

These cases and dozens of our own would certainly suggest that physicians have badly neglected the role of adequate record-taking. If patients are going to avoid a lot of unnecessary examinations, tests, pain and expense, they have to be a great deal more candid about their coffee intake. That is to say that doctors will have to start *asking* more coffee consumption questions and patients are going to have to start *volunteering* more information as well.

Neither is occurring at this time, to the detriment of the patient.

And that's happening largely because neither doctor nor patient are fully aware of the great variety of abnormalities which are caused by coffee consumption. The central nervous system, in fact, is just one and perhaps one of the lesser casualties in the great war between coffee and your mind and body. A more deadly prognosis is lurking just beyond.

6

Coffee And The Big C

Welcome, now, to the most frightening of all possible prognoses from the coffee addiction: Cancer.

More than half the population over the age of ten drinks coffee. Average per capita rate: Two cups per day. The average *coffee drinker* puts away 3-4 cups per day. Upwards of 30,000,000 drinkers polish off at least 5 and up to 25 or more cups per day. You can imagine the shock value of announcing that coffee causes cancer.

But does coffee *cause* cancer? Nobody knows that for sure, yet. But a mounting body of evidence is suggesting that if you want to avoid certain cancers, you are well-advised to kick the coffee habit.

The latest volley in the controversy was fired recently by a group of Harvard researchers who studied the effects of coffee drinking on 369 hospital patients and reached this conclusion: There is an 80 percent higher risk of pancreatic cancer associated with drinking two cups of coffee daily. Translated another way, that means that some 75 million coffee drinkers are exposing themselves to the pain, suffering and possible death due to pancreatic cancer because of their coffee drinking. That is the risk at the *lower* levels of coffee drinking. The potential gets markedly greater the more coffee you drink.[1]

Take a look at the bad news.

Number of Cups Daily	Increased Risk
1-2	2.1 times
2	2.7 times
3-4	2.8 times
5 or more	3.2 times

To put it another way, virtually *every one* of the 200 plus coffee drinkers in our survey (coffee drinkers who have now quit), were more than three times as likely to get pancreatic cancer than those people who didn't drink coffee. And maybe they still are.

Does that sound startling? You bet it does!

Or, try this one out. Combining figures from the National Coffee Association and the Harvard research group, the *average* U.S. coffee drinker is consuming coffee at a rate which nearly *triples* his risk of pancreatic cancer.

I think those figures are absolutely out of sight!

As a matter of fact, it was so overwhelming to some coffee drinkers in our sample that the cancer scare was the single most important precipitating factor in their quitting. Fully 10 percent of our coffee quitters said the "fear of cancer" was what motivated them into kicking the habit for good.

What Is Pancreatic Cancer?

The pancreas is one of your body's most vital organs and is situated just behind the stomach. The 7-inch-long, fish-shaped organ secretes digestive enzymes into the small intestine that help the body turn food into energy. While it is not one of the most prevalent of cancers in the U.S., it certainly is one of the deadliest.

Survival is Slim

Cancer of the pancreas has the highest fatality rate of all cancers. Only about three percent of those who develop pancreatic cancer are alive three years after diagnosis, only two percent after five years.

The American Cancer Society has provided these somber statistical estimates for cancer during 1981. You can do your own computing to determine which of these cancers you'd least like to get:

Cancer	Cases	Deaths	Percent
Lung	122,000	105,000	86
Colon-Rectum	120,000	54,900	46
Breast	110,000	37,100	33
Prostate	70,000	22,700	32
Pancreas	24,200	22,000	91

Cancer of the pancreas, it can be seen, is the country's fifth most common form of cancer. It strikes men slightly more often than women. But worst of all, if you're stricken with pancreatic cancer, you're likely to die from it—and soon.

The link between coffee drinking and pancreatic cancer cannot be taken lightly—even though great numbers of present-day coffee drinkers are likely to do so. Disbelief, of course, has always been a great hindrance to behavior modifications and I would expect coffee drinking and cancer statistics to be no different.

It's been over 15 years since the Surgeon General's famous report was issued, linking cigarette smoking with heart disease, lung cancer, emphysema, and a great number of other diseases, both crippling and fatal. Certainly, many smokers studied this information and came to believe they were significantly shortening their lives if they continued to smoke.

But millions more did not. At least 50,000,000 people are still smoking cigarettes in the U.S. They either don't believe the awful truth or they don't care. I don't know which is worse.

The Harvard Study

The Harvard Study involved 1,013 patients in 11 large hospitals in Boston and Rhode Island. Data was obtained on the smoking and drinking habits of 369 people with diagnosed pancreatic cancer and 644 patients hospitalized with other diseases.

What the researchers found was not at all what they were looking for.

The researchers set out to see if there was a link between this form of cancer and cigarette or alcohol use. What they found was that the use of alcoholic beverages did not significantly relate to any increase in pancreatic cancer. They also drew a blank on associating increased cancer risks with the use of tea, pipe tobacco, or cigars.

Then came the surprise. The data did show "a consistent association of pancreatic cancer with coffee drinking within each category of smoking, and the data for all smokers and non-smokers showed a consistent trend with coffee drinking after adjustment for smoking."

The findings of the Harvard group are consistent with previous investigations which also showed an association between coffee drinking and pancreatic cancer.

In another case-control study involving 94 patients, the researchers found that patients with pancreatic adenocarcinoma tended to drink more decaffeinated coffee than did those in the control group.

Coffee Or Caffeine?

The Harvard study not only pointed an accusing finger at regular coffee, but cast a specter on decaffeinated coffee as well because the researchers failed to find any link between pancreatic cancer and *tea* drinking. Presumably, such a finding would rule out any link between caffeine and pancreatic cancer because tea also contains caffeine. Thus, it appears that whether you drink decaffeinated or regular coffee, you still share the increased risk of pancreatic cancer—according to researchers.

The Harvard researchers disagreed somewhat, with findings about decaffeinated coffee reached earlier by a group of Maryland researchers.

In that study,[2] it was found that "habitual consumption of decaffeinated coffee was significantly *greater* among pancreatic cancer patients than controls." The study also noted that the chemical tricholorethylene (TCE), once widely used to decaffeinate coffee, is the same chemical that was used to dry clean clothes. Men in the dry cleaning business, they found, had an increased risk of pancreatic cancer.

The Harvard researchers believed, however, "in view of the relatively recent use of decaffeinated coffee on a large scale, it seems unlikely that this particular type of beverage has a causal relation to cases of pancreatic cancer appearing at present. It seems more likely," they said, "that the high consumption of decaffeinated coffee is really a reflection of generally high coffee consumption by these patients in the past."

Decaffeinated Coffee and Cancer

Decaffeinated coffee has been around for nearly 75 years, the result of an ironic twist of fate and a young German doctor.

Dr. Ludwig Roselius, in 1890, patented the rather simple decaffeinating process in response to what he believed was the premature death of his father, a coffee merchant and coffee taster. Roselius believed his father was killed by the excessive amounts of caffeine he ingested, and he may have been right.

Following the patent of the decaffeinating process Roselius set up a business using his method. The company was based in Bremen, Germany. His product was Sanka, a rather simple, but brilliant abbreviation from the French, "sans caffeine."

The Roselius process spread to this country in the early 1900s where it was acquired by the General Foods Corporation.

Roselius's method was simple: he merely heated the unroasted coffee beans with steam to raise their moisture level, then he used a chemical to extract the caffeine. The beans were then washed, steamed, dried, then roasted and ground for consumption.[3]

While certain refinements have been made to the process, it remains much the same, except for the chemicals used to extract the caffeine.

The TCE Cancer Scare

TCE was the most widely used chemical until the 1970s when the National Cancer Institute dropped a bomb into the laps of coffee processors: TCE, they reported, can cause cancer of the liver in laboratory mice. That memorandum, sent coffee makers scampering for safer chemicals. Companies stopped using the TCE in July 1975. And while no formal action has been taken to ban TCE from foods, drugs and other products, the FDA is awaiting further information on the safety of this chemical.

The FDA has ruled, however, that the residue of methylene chloride, the chemical now used to decaffeinate beans, must not exceed 10 parts per million.

Dr. Brian MacMahon, who led the Harvard research group, said the association between coffee drinking and pancreatic cancer ought to be evaluated with other data.

Said MacMahon, "If it (the association) reflects a causal relation between coffee drinking and pancreatic cancer, coffee use might account for a substantial portion of the cases of this disease in the U.S."

"If the distribution of coffee consumption in our control group reflects that in the general population ... we estimate the proportion of pancreatic cancer that is potentially attributable to coffee consumption to be slightly more than 50 percent."

In short, MacMahon is saying that if the link between coffee and pancreatic cancer is a valid one, then at least 10,000 lives might be saved each year if the victims had not drank coffee!

MacMahon, who used to be a three-cup-a-day drinker, believes in what he says. When the results became known, MacMahon kicked the coffee habit.

The Pancreas And Hypoglycemia

One of the least researched ailments of excessive coffee consumption is a curiosity known as hypoglycemia. I say curiosity because many medical professionals think the hypoglycemia theory is sheer quackery and there is no solid evidence as to exactly what causes this condition and how coffee consumption could either create or aggravate it.

About all that is known, for sure, is what it is: an abnormally low concentration of sugar in the blood. Beyond that, little is known.

Hypoglycemia is determined, in part, by the blood sugar or glucose level in your body. While less than two teaspoonsful of glucose are normally in your blood, excess sugar is stored in your liver. When too much sugar builds up in your blood, the pancreas pumps out extra insulin to help the body assimilate it. Some doctors believe that in some people, too much insulin is pumped out and too much sugar is removed. The result, they say, is low blood sugar, or hypoglycemia.

According to these theorists, hypoglycemics suffer from jitteriness, sweating, rapid heart beats, weakness and even fainting spells. Hypoglycemics also suffer from blurred vision, headaches, dullness, confusions, etc.

Sound familiar? It should. It sounds a great deal like the sort of central nervous system disorders that millions of American coffee drinkers are suffering from every day.

And here's where the kicker comes in. Some doctors believe that caffeine-containing beverages like coffee and colas—release stored body sugar into the bloodstream.

When hypoglycemics drink caffeine-containing beverages like coffee and colas—extra blood sugar is released into their bloodstreams and the punishment begins. The extra sugar at first makes them feel good—but eventually it just makes their blood sugar level drop even lower. The result, in short, is a continual mood swing produced by coffee consumption—a mood swing whose origin the unknowing hypoglycemic is entirely unaware.

One of the doctors who has studied the problem suggests that many people who experience migraine headaches, panic attacks and other symptoms, ought to look first to their coffee consumption for the answer.

"It makes you wonder about the caffeine and sugar intake in their diets. The trouble is that many doctors and researchers just won't want to believe something as simple as caffeine or sugar might be at the root of so many problems."[4]

Coffee Drinking and Bladder Cancer

Other cancers may also be linked with coffee consumption, as a variety of studies have shown, particularly cancer of the bladder.

Cancer of the urinary bladder has long been recognized as a hazard of environmental exposure to certain chemicals.[5] Likewise, cigarette smoking increases the risk of developing this cancer, particularly in male smokers. Still, a significant number of bladder cancer cases remained unexplained by tobacco use or exposure to chemicals—cancers which may be linked to coffee drinking.

In a Canadian population-based case-control study,[6] 480 pairs of male patients and 152 pairs of female patients and controls were selected and interviewed about their use of certain substances including cigarettes, coffee, non-public water supplies, and their exposure to certain industrial chemicals. The patients had newly diagnosed cases of bladder cancer.

What the study revealed was that not only was coffee drinking associated with increased risk of bladder cancer, but the drinking of non-diet cola drinks also was linked.

The increased risk among men was about 1.5 times for regular and instant coffee users and about 1.4 for all types of coffee. The relationship with other beverages was not statistically significant.

Here's a rundown of the increased risk these Canadian researchers discovered:

2 cups per day	1.6
3-4 cups per day	1.3
More than 4 cups per day	1.5

Strangely enough, instant coffee proved even more dangerous than the regular coffees. But taken as a whole, the increased risk of bladder cancer was not dose-related. That is, drinking more coffee did not materially increase the chances of developing the cancer.

The findings parallel several other studies on coffee consumption and bladder cancer which suggested that coffee is definitely associated with bladder cancer, but the dose required to significantly alter the statistics has not been determined.

Further research will, no doubt, shed additional light on how coffee drinking is related to bladder cancer and cancers of all types.

Unexplained Skin Lesions

One of the puzzling aspects of our research was the number of unexplained cases of skin lesions which—although not directly related to skin cancers—could be.

Take the case of a 55-year-old North Dakota man who told us he drank coffee because "it was something to do with my hands" but gave it up because of a lesion on his face that simply refused to heal itself—until he kicked the habit.

The man drank about five cups of coffee daily for some 40 years before giving it up.

"I had a lesion on my face and I experimented with dropping various things from my diet. When I quit drinking coffee, the lesion went away," he said.

The lesion appeared as a scaly patch next to his nose and under his eye. The doctor diagnosed the ailment as seborrhea, which is an excess discharge from the sebaceous gland.

"It was gone just like that," he said after quitting his coffee consumption. "I'm definite on that. It was caused by my coffee drinking and (the scales) disappeared so dramatically when I quit."

●

Another much younger respondent, this one a woman of 22, reported an identical experience. She had been drinking about two to three cups of coffee for about two years before she became concerned about the "cancer scare." She had no other strong reasons for quitting. But when she did, she was amazed to find that a skin lesion around her nose miraculously disappeared. She had suffered from the scaly facial blemish for years. And now that she has quit—it has never reappeared.

●

Who knows precisely what ingredient in coffee caused this disease. And who can say for sure how many thousands, even millions of other Americans are suffering from similar afflictions. Future research may give us the answers.

In the meantime, health-conscious Americans such as the coffee quitters in our research, are leading the way. They're discovering that their new dietary measures can significantly improve appearance, health and well-being. And it's likely that the results of their "research", their self-prescriptions of coffee- and caffeine-free diets, will lead the way to much of the professional research when and if it occurs.

The important thing to remember right now is this: coffee drinking—whether regular, decaffeinated or instant—is linked to pancreatic and bladder cancers. And the smart money would bet that the association is going to become stronger as more research is completed. Therefore, if you want to live a longer, healthier life, get wise and get with it. Kick the coffee habit now!

7

Coffee and Your Heart

Charlotte is a 57-year-old coffee drinker who had drank up to a dozen cups of coffee every morning for the past 40 years. Like many other heavy coffee drinkers, she occasionally had problems with her coffee drinking, sleepless nights, nervousness and the like. But by and large, she suffered no pronounced physical problems that she could readily identify as being *caused* by her coffee drinking.

Until her heart began to act strangely.

In the middle of one of her morning coffee drinking binges, her heart began to beat both faster and irregularly. At first, she was alarmed, but thought the condition would subside. It didn't. Instead, it persisted all day long. By the next day, the fluttering heartbeat disappeared. But it mysteriously appeared at least once or twice a week.

Despite regular checkups, she reported that her doctor had *never* inquired about her coffee consumption. When her persistent heartbeat irregularities brought her to the doctor's doorstep again, she was hospitalized—and still her personal physician knew not to ask the most important question.

During her hospital stay, however, a heart specialist did inquire about her caffeine consumption and when it was learned that she was putting away a dozen cups each day, she was immediately prohibited from drinking coffee and was given other medication to stabilize her wayward heartbeat. Following her break from the coffee habit, the heart irregularities disappeared. Charlotte is now a happy, healthier woman *without* the coffee habit. She may have even saved her life.

●

Each year Americans consume more than two *billion* pounds of coffee—an enormous gluttony which affects both their morbidity and their mortality.

It disrupts many organs and tissues of the body, not the least of which is your heart—although no one has proved that coffee consumption *causes* heart disease.

When caffeine is taken into your system, it is absorbed easily from the gastrointestinal tract and quickly finds its way into the central nervous system.

Within minutes, depending on the amount of caffeine consumed, the heart muscle is disturbed.

Caffeine is a myocardial (heart muscle) stimulant and with heavy caffeine consumption, such stimulation can cause cardiac irregularities which, in turn, can cause death!

With just two or three cups of coffee, blood pressure can increase by as much as 14 percent. Cardiac muscles stimulated by caffeine increase the force of contraction, heart rate and cardiac output. The result can either increase or decrease the rate at which the heart beats.

Caffeine dilates the coronary, pulmonary and general systemic blood vessels by causing a relaxation of the smooth muscle in the vessel walls.

Let there be no question. When you drink coffee, your heart often has to work harder. And because it does work harder, doctors have long thought that coffee may be involved in heart disease.

What The Studies Say

One of the interesting studies which has been done was performed at University of Minnesota Laboratory of Physiological Hygiene. It has some important news for coffee drinkers who already have heart disease, and even for those who don't.

The study included 7,300 men aged 35 to 57 who had healthy hearts at the time of the research. The group was questioned on how much coffee they drank, how much alcohol they consumed, their smoking habits—even how much sleep they got.

What the study showed was that heavy coffee drinkers are more likely to develop what doctors call VPBs (ventricular premature beat), an irregular off-rhythm heart beat.

VPBs are not terribly important in and of themselves. People with healthy hearts can get them, and they won't kill you if you're healthy, or at least have a healthy *heart*. But for patients with heart disease, the VPBs have been linked with heart attacks and even death.

Even more important is this crucial question: just how many thousands, or even millions of people with *undisclosed* heart problems are *right today* drinking 5, 10 or even 15 cups of coffee per day? Can you declare, with absolute certainty, that *your* heart is perfectly normal? Probably not, unless you've just had a complete physical. But most Americans have not. Thus the risk is there—and it is waiting.

But even those coffee drinkers who do not have heart disease ought to be concerned about their coffee consumption and the way it affects their heart.

A dietician and long-time coffee drinker (45 years), told us that she began to suffer from heart palpitations. One of her friends "suggested" she give up coffee to relieve the problem. She did, and the palpitations disappeared.

Other coffee drinkers who develop high blood pressure and its sometimes fatal complications, look to kicking the coffee habit as a way to reduce the risk. A number of respondents in our survey did so.

"I was troubled with high blood pressure and my doctor advised me to quit coffee," said a middle-aged woman. After she quit drinking coffee she reported, "My blood pressure is normal now and I'm sure it had a lot to do with the caffeine." The woman takes no other drugs for the problem.

A 60-year-old machinist reported that he had been hospitalized a couple of times for heart palpitations. He found that his condition was related to his coffee consumption, and it did not matter whether the coffee was regular or decaffeinated. He quit both and his heart has functioned normally ever since.

As nettlesome as these heart disturbances are, their significance pales when compared to the more dangerous cardiac abnormalities including coronary heart disease.

Heart Disease

During the past 20 years, a number of studies have been conducted charting the risk factors of chronic degenerative heart disease. The results produced a mixed picture.

One of the premier studies of heavy coffee drinking and myocardial infarctions showed a definite link between the two— enough so that even the most avowed coffee lover might seek a separation.

Myocardial infarction is the degeneration of the heart muscle tissue that results when the tissue's blood supply is restricted by clogged or blocked blood vessels.

This particular study[2] showed that the risk of developing this disease is about *twice* as great for heavy coffee drinkers as it is for individuals who drink no coffee at all.

The two researchers, Hershel Jick and Dennis Slone, undertook two studies. The first compared 276 myocardial infarction patients from eight hospitals in the U.S., Canada, New Zealand,

and Israel, with more than a thousand control patients with other diseases. A second study compared 440 patients from 24 Boston-area hospitals with more than 12,000 patients with other diseases.

In each study, they found that patients who drank one to five cups of coffee daily ran an approximately 50 percent greater risk of developing this heart disease than did those who drank no coffee. Patients who drank six or more cups daily ran a risk which was 110 percent higher.

Coffee Was To Blame

Another interesting note on the Jick and Slone study was that the heavy tea drinkers did not run the same risk as heavy coffee drinkers. In effect, then, caffeine was exonerated from suspicion—just as caffeine was "cleared" of being associated with pancreatic cancer.

Thus, you're just as likely to develop pancreatic cancer or myocardial infarction by drinking regular or decaffeinated coffee.

As you might expect, however, several other conditions can increase this type of heart disease. The increased risk was greatest, for example, among patients who were already predisposed toward the development of the disease by variables which included diabetes, certain occupations, cigarette smoking, age and sex.

The *source* of the link between coffee drinking and myocardial infarction remains a mystery. For that reason, the results of these researchers have been criticized. The study was criticized even more strongly because the conclusion was based on a retrospective study, that is, one in which the evidence was gathered from patients who *already had* the disease.

Still other studies found no link whatsoever between coffee drinking and heart disease. The best known of these studies was the Framingham Heart Disease Epidemiology Study which was conducted under the sponsorship of the National Institute of Health.[3]

More than 5,100 adult residents of Framingham, Mass. were monitored for nearly 20 years in an attempt to find any link between dietary, physiological and environmental and personality traits and heart disease. That report showed no link whatsoever.

Other studies have found that coffee drinking is related to increased levels of heart disease only when the coffee habit is joined by another dangerous habit: cigarette smoking.[4] [5]

A study in Evans County, Georgia, found no association with coffee usage, even though that section of the U.S. has been called a "stroke belt" because of its high incidence of stroke victims.[6]

Still another study, this one a "total adult population" study from Finland, showed an appreciable effect of heavy coffee consumption on the prevalence of myocardial infarction and coronary heart disease death.

Conclusions

Despite the wide ranging and often conflicting results from these studies, a number of conclusions can be drawn from this and other data.

- **Caffeine has a profound effect on the heart and has been shown to cause heart palpitations, ventricular premature beats, extra systoles, abnormally fast and slow heart beats.**
- **Coffee has been associated with both low and high blood pressure.**
- **Coffee—whether regular or decaffeinated—has been associated in some studies with myocardial infarction.**
- **Persons with a history of heart disease ought to avoid coffee and caffeinated beverages because these substances can pose a significant hazard to their health and longevity.**

- Persons who are predisposed to heart disease, those who are overweight or smoke, for example, ought to avoid coffee and caffeine because they increase their risk of heart problems in greater degrees than those who do not drink coffee.
- While further research is necessary to determine the reason why coffee may lead to heart problems, the prudent, health-conscious public should kick the habit now—before it's too late.

8

A Gut Reaction About Coffee

Frances is a 41-year-old office manager who began her slide into coffee addiction some 23 years ago. At age 18, she began to drink coffee daily, although in amounts which seldom exceeded a cup or two per day.

But as she got older, married, and had children, the coffee pot "was always on" during her at-home maternity sojourns and when she returned to work her consumption continued at the new higher levels.

Now after bearing three children, her addiction reached daylong drinking levels and a mysterious pain began occurring in her stomach.

"Some days it was there. Some days it wasn't," she said. And because it waxed and waned without apparent reason, the cause of the pain remained obscure.

For fully nine years these pains came and went, until 1979 when they grew decidedly worse and more frequent. Even so, the *cause* remained a mystery. Some days when she drank a great deal of coffee, anywhere from 5 to 10 cups, the pain was nowhere to be found. Then, a couple of days *later*, and from out of nowhere, the pain would appear. So violent were these pains that even after the pain itself would subside, her stomach muscles ached for days while they recovered.

Seeking relief, Frances went to her doctor and described the pains. "They are simply terrible," she told him. "I get these atrocious stomach aches, gas pains, knots in my stomach, that burning feeling." The doctor told her to go to the hospital where a number of stomach tests were performed but they didn't find anything. "My doctor told me I might be 'pre-ulcer', but said there was nothing wrong with me, that I was perfectly OK and there was nothing we can do for you," she repeated.

The woman complained that she was doubled over with stomach pains, that there *must* be something wrong. Still, she got no medication, no advice.

Undaunted, Frances tried her own prescription. She had a sneaking suspicion that her coffee drinking might have something to do with the pain and decided to quit.

In a couple of days, the pain disappeared. And in more than two years, they have never returned.

•

If you think Frances's story is unique, you're greatly mistaken. Fully 37 percent of the coffee quitters in our sample cited gastrointestinal problems as the major reason why they decided to chuck the coffee habit. Nearly 50 percent said they were at least "troubled" by stomach problems including many coffee drinkers who drank as few as one or two cups per day.

Again, it was not unusual to find coffee drinkers who performed their own gastrointestinal self-diagnosis—without (or even in spite of) a doctor's recommendation.

"I started getting these terrific headaches on the weekend," said a 27-year-old payroll supervisor. "Then I'd get these terrible stomach pains if I drank coffee on an empty stomach. When I quit drinking coffee they went away. I haven't had any since."

A 58-year-old engineer, a 20-year coffee drinking veteran, began having stomach trouble due to the seven or eight cups of coffee he was drinking daily. "I knew that if I would go to the doctor, he'd send me to the hospital for checkups and everything," he said. "Eventually, I'd just end up spending a lot of money and he'd tell me to quit drinking coffee. So I took it upon myself and quit."

The engineer said it took four full weeks for the withdrawal symptoms to disappear, but when they did, so did his stomach pains.

There is no need to demonstrate to this group of quitters that coffee was *responsible* for their distresses. They know it. They needed no research report, no newspaper article, to convince them.

Coffee and Peptic Ulcers

There is ample research that suggests coffee is causally linked to peptic ulcers and even greater evidence that once you have developed such an ulcer, coffee is about the worst thing you can feed it.

In one of the earliest studies[1] of coffee consumption and peptic ulcers, a group of researchers tested the gastric secretory response of 36 patients with peptic ulcers and 50 subjects without ulcers. The results were dramatic. They learned that not only does caffeine and coffee stimulate gastric secretion, but they also found that the excessive use of caffeine-containing beverages may contribute to the *development* of peptic ulcers in ulcer-susceptible persons. Further, they found that those patients who develop peptic ulcers have a much more difficult time controlling the disease if they continue to drink coffee.

They also learned that Sanka and other decaffeinated coffees also stimulate the secretion of gastric acids. Not only are decaffeinated coffees found to be responsible for this dangerous over-secretion of stomach juices, but coffee *substitutes* were found guilty as well. The report suggested that coffee stimulates gastric secretion because of its caffeine content and because of other agents: natural, roast products or irritant volatile oils. Thus, all roasted grain beverages were found to be hazardous, not just coffee.

The report also pointed out that caffeine and caffeine-containing beverages provoke a prolonged increase in the total output of acid by the stomach in patients with peptic ulcers.

In view of all this, the report urged that those persons with peptic ulcers or those who are predisposed to such ulcers refrain from drinking coffee and caffeinated beverages. This is particularly true, the report said of their excessive use.

The study ended on a rather peculiar note, however, suggestive of the sort of insanity that sometimes goes on in medical circles. "It is realized," the paper said, "that the psychological hardship of total abstinence is sometimes more aggravating to the ulcer patient than the pharmacodynamic effects of a contraindicated substance. In such instances, the report concludes, "a single cup of coffee with sugar and milk or cream with the meal could be allowed."

Imagine that. Here we've got learned researchers telling us that there are coffee addicts around who are so hooked on their drug that the psychological pain of not having their fix is greater than the real physical pain from peptic ulcers. And these clinicians, in their "wisdom", suggest that it's better to *perpetuate* the addiction than to kick the habit and live a healthier life.

Tell me about the wisdom of that medical advice.

Heartburn and Coffee

Heartburn. That burning sensation beneath the breastbone that happens when a spastic backflow of acid stomach contents flows into the esophagus. Millions of Americans get it all the time. It's a frequent companion of a significant portion of heavy coffee drinkers, perhaps as many as 40 to 50 percent.

Presumably, this backflow is caused by an increase or a decrease in lower esophageal sphincter pressure (LESP). Without getting into the technical jargon doctors use, the sphincter is a muscle which can open and close the port between the stomach and the esophagus. The exact relationship between coffee and LESP is yet to be determined.

The pain, often accompanied by gas and diarrhea, is made worse by position, certain foods—and over all else—coffee.

Study after study has confirmed that such heartburn is linked to excessive use of coffee. And "excessive" can be just about any amount—depending on the individual. Some coffee drinkers report such distress after only a cup or two. Other coffee drinkers consume five or ten cups of coffee a day—and only begin to feel the symptoms.

In an interesting study of the heartburn problem, Dr. Sidney Cohen tested 57 persons who had reduced their coffee intake because of gastrointestinal problems. Most of the study subjects (65 percent) had reduced their coffee intake. Some 35 percent had quit entirely.

Upon reintroducing coffee into their systems through nasogastric tubes, it was found that almost 50 percent suffered from gas, (ranging from bloating, belching and passage of flatus). Thirty-nine patients suffered from diarrhea. Nine percent of the patients complained of chest pains and about 11 percent cited nausea.[2]

Interestingly enough, these numbers roughly parallel those of our own research, gathered in the same way but measured through recall. The former coffee drinkers who responded to our research suffered from all of these ailments, in about the same percentages. The only difference was that they had not *reintroduced* coffee into their systems. They had merely eliminated it.

The study suggested that short of changing the chemical makeup of coffee, persons who experience coffee-induced stomach problems have no way to avoid them—except by quitting coffee altogether. "Since the (heartburn) symptoms can be modified by reduction in acid secretion alone," the report said, "this goal may be sought in a coffee product. (But) previous studies suggested that decaffeination does *not* achieve this goal since it alters acid secretion only minimally."[3]

The concluding note to this study is that coffee may *cause* or *aggravate* heartburn and this is true whether your coffee is decaffeinated or not.

More Evidence

Another study came up with the same result, although it found that coffee *lowers* the sphincter pressure, not increases it.[4]

In this report, volunteer subjects drank coffee and were later tested for heartburn symptoms. Again, the patients were found to significantly increase their heartburn symptoms after drinking coffee—even though nobody has, as yet, put the finger on precisely *why* this occurs.

Obviously, future research will have to determine the exact link between coffee consumption and gastrointestinal disorders. For right now, however, the knowledge that coffee—whether decaffeinated or not—causes these problems ought to be significant enough to kick the habit.

How Much Coffee Wrecks Your Stomach?

Most of the coffee quitters in our survey drank somewhere around eight cups of coffee a day—a little more than twice what the average coffee drinker nationwide drinks.

Some coffee drinkers began complaining about the effects of coffee with as few as one cup per day. Others didn't start complaining—or quitting—until they reached the higher levels, say 10 to 15 cups per day.

But interestingly enough, those persons who quit primarily because it was extremely distressful to their gastrointestinal systems drank little more than anyone else in our survey. That is, around eight cups a day.

Sure, there were people who suffered from ulcers, stomach cramps, etc., who drank as little as three to five cups a day. And there were many who drank upwards of 20 cups a day. But most were drinking anywhere from three to eight cups a day.

And seeing the national *average* among coffee drinkers is around three to four cups per day, we're obviously a nation of coffee drinkers who are begging for stomach troubles—now and in the future. After all, today's three-cup-per-day drinker might well be tomorrow's four- or five-cup drinker. Today's experimenters are tomorrow's addicts.

Perhaps more important than the *amount* of coffee you drink each day is the *length of time* you have been excessively drinking coffee.

While disturbances of the heart, lungs, and central nervous system seem to be fairly evenly distributed throughout our group of respondents, regardless of age, stomach disorders were not.

These gastrointestinal problems appeared more likely to occur among coffee drinkers who have been drinking excessive amounts of coffee for much longer periods of time.

The risks of severe stomach disorders, in fact, seems to increase in direct proportion to the number of years the respondent drank coffee.

A doctor in our research suggested that because the oils and acids in coffee irritate the stomach linings, tissues which are continually insulted by these chemicals will, over time, begin to inflame and become painful. While in most coffee drinkers it takes many years of such insults to cause this inflamation, excessive coffee drinking over many years will predictably lead to this result.

In our study we could almost predict that if the respondent had been drinking six or more cups of coffee a day for more than 20 years, he would almost invariably report that "stomach problems" were the principle reason why he kicked the habit.

Thus, if there is any predictive value in our coffee addiction statistics, we can clearly suggest that at least 50,000,000 American coffee drinkers are risking serious stomach problems through their coffee drinking habit of five cups a day. The prognosis is substantially poorer for the 21,000,000 who drink six or more cups a day. Perhaps up to 50 percent and more could be stricken with serious stomach problems. It's a stark prognosis, at best. And a terrifying one at worst.

9

Special Risks For Females

If men and women equally shared the increased health risk due to coffee drinking, the world might be a fairer place in which to live. But life is not fair.

Women are getting a bum rap. Women suffer from coffee-related pathologies far more than men. The diseases and ailments are greater in *number*. They are greater in *degree*. They are far greater in their implications for present and future societies.

There are reasons for this unequal burden. Certainly, because women generally weigh less than men, they are more profoundly affected by similar amounts of coffee. The same is true for children. Because kids weigh substantially less than adults, their body weight is more greatly affected by given levels of caffeine. For example, the caffeine in a single bottle or can of cola drink can equal the caffeine dosage of four cups of coffee drank by an adult.

Research shows that more women than men complain about coffee related illnesses and diseases. Moreover, women often report they endure a greater degree of pain and suffering from these pathologies than men. But most significantly, women report they suffer from a larger number of ailments because many of the diseases associated with coffee drinking are female related. And finally, women appear to kick the coffee habit in much greater numbers than men because of the unequal burden they seek to disown.

A case in point is our own research on more than 200 persons who had quit drinking coffee. Women outnumbered men in our sample of "coffee quitters" by more than 2 to 1. Moreover, the variety of their complaints greatly exceeded those reported by males.

Women suffered from withdrawal to a greater degree than men; their withdrawal generally lasted longer, and their symptoms were more pronounced than in men.

But the single most salient fact is this: women suffer from a greater number of the more serious medical problems than men.

Because Women Are Women

Coffee consumed by humans, both female and male, takes the same physiological course: the caffeine is easily absorbed from the gastrointestinal tract and is rapidly distributed to all tissues and organs of the body. Research has established that each tissue bears caffeine about in proportion to the tissue's water content.

That caffeine flows easily to all parts of the body is bad enough. That it flows to vital tissues in the *female* body is a great deal worse.

The ovaries and the fetus in the womb are bathed in caffeine shortly after the drug is ingested. In men, the testes also are subjected to caffeine leading some researchers to believe that it causes male infertility. This phenomena presents a clear and present danger to the unborn. Caffeine also appears in the milk of mothers who breastfeed their newborns. But the most frightening evidence is that caffeine could cause birth defects.

The First Cautionary Note

From a historical perspective, geneticists first reported in 1948 that caffeine produced mutations in certain bacteria and fungi. As the years passed, reports of caffeine-related genetic malfunctions began to creep up the biological ladder. In the early 50s, other studies began confirming the notion that caffeine causes important biological changes. Researchers learned that caffeine caused chromosome breaks or losses in cultured human cancer cells. The same effect was noted in human white blood cells.

And while there have been many studies on the effect of caffeine consumption by mothers of children with birth defects, most studies now point to the possibility that caffeine may endanger the human fetus.[1]

The best known study to date, and the one which has caused considerable worry for pregnant mothers, was conducted recently by the FDA.[2]

The study was conducted under the direction of Dr. Thomas F. X. Collins. Although the research was conducted on rats, it revealed much damning evidence against coffee in the form of hideous birth defects. The most common birth defect the research noted was the improper formation or total absence of digits on paws of the offspring. The research also found that delayed bone development, particularly the breastbone, occurred, although this abnormality was thought not to be permanent. The fetal abnormalities occurred when the rats were given caffeine in an amount equivalent to human doses of as little as two cups and as many as 24 cups.

Keep in mind here that probably 15,000,000 to 20,000,000 Americans drink five or more cups per day. There are at least 100,000 pregnant women and probably many more, who drink at least nine cups per day.[3]

When this report was issued, many researchers and coffee experts stressed that there is no evidence linking coffee and birth defects *in humans*. Although the FDA study is regarded as an excellent, well-controlled experiment, they said, it still only confirmed that caffeine causes birth defects in rats—not in humans. Man is not a big rat, the skeptics said, as they waited for more "proof."

But other coffee watchers knew better. And one was the Center For Science In The Public Interest (CSPI).

In a landmark case, reported by CSPI, a Virginia Beach, Va. girl was the victim of birth defects identical to those seen in the FDA and other studies, birth defects which CSPI said "were almost certainly caused by the mother's heavy coffee consumption during pregnancy."

According to CSPI, the mother drank 10 to 12 cups of coffee a day during pregnancy, although she avoided alcohol, tobacco and over-the-counter medications which might have caused birth defects.

"I never took so much as one aspirin during my pregnancy," the woman told a Washington, D.C. press conference, "I was so concerned that a drug might hurt the baby."

The woman went on to report that "I hope that my experience will benefit the thousands of pregnant women who drink a lot of coffee. Even aside from my case and the animal studies, it just makes common sense to avoid caffeine along with all other unnecessary drugs during pregnancy. When the risk is as serious as a birth defect, we should certainly err on the side of caution."

CSPI, a 15,000 member Washington D.C.-based group which works primarily on diet and health issues, is taking the fight against caffeine and birth defects several additional steps. CSPI has formed a clearinghouse for information on caffeine caused birth defects. The group has asked that women whose daily consumption during pregnancy was five cups of coffee or more to contact the center, particularly if they also avoided other drugs.

The center was able to turn up several more mothers whose coffee drinking, they said, was related to birth defects in their children. All three drank upwards of 12 cups of coffee a day, but did not expose themselves to other agents which might cause birth defects.

Children of the three were born with missing fingers and toes. The report was published in Lancet, a leading British medical journal.

The organization, because of such damning evidence, has written to major coffee producers urging them to voluntarily place a warning notice on their coffee labels.

While there is little chance that the coffee producers will follow CSPI's recommendation, perhaps the government will follow through.

Rep. Andrew Maguire (Dem.-N.J.) has called on the FDA to require warning labels on coffee and tea and to mount an educational campaign so that developing embryos would not be exposed to caffeine.[4]

Maguire said, "The government needs to develop a clear and consistent policy on chemicals that cause birth defects as soon as possible, if we are to avoid a tragedy such as Britain, Germany, and other countries experienced with thalidomide."

Thalidomide, you may recall, was the sedative used back in the 1960s. It was widely used by Europeans. When taken by women, it produced severe birth deformities in babies, including missing or deformed arms and legs.

Cautionary alarms have also been sounded in the New York offices of the March of Dimes, which disseminated a fact sheet that counseled women to avoid excessive coffee use during pregnancy. By "excessive," the national medical organization meant six or more cups per day. The publication was sent to March of Dimes chapters and medical science reporters throughout the U.S.

"Although caffeine has yet to be established as a toxic to a human fetus, any drug," the March of Dimes warned, "that crosses the placenta (as caffeine does) may be regarded as possibly hazardous, especially during the first three months of pregnancy."

And just how big of a problem are we talking about? I guess it depends on whose baby it is. Each year, some 200,000 babies in the U.S. are born with birth defects. An additional 560,000 conceptions result in stillbirths, miscarriages or infant death, due to defective fetal development. Couple that with a high percentage of natural abortuses that are malformed, and you have a problem of considerable importance. It is a problem which is crucially important not just to pregnant women, but all women and all mankind.

According to the March of Dimes, an increased incidence of breech deliveries, poor muscle tone, low birthweight, stillbirths, miscarriages, premature birth and newborns who just "look abnormal" have been suggested in preliminary, unpublished studies on the effects of caffeine on the human fetus. Other studies, say the foundation, suggest no such effects.

What Caffeine May Be Doing

The March of Dimes Defects Foundation continually monitors and evaluates studies of the effects of caffeine on the human fetus.

The reason caffeine is so potentially dangerous, according to the foundation is that caffeine may be a mutagen (gene-damaging agent) and perhaps a teratogen (cause of abnormal development). That's because its chemical structure, similar to one of the constituents of DNA, is believed to enter every cell, including the fetal gonads.

One theory, according to the foundation, is that caffeine acts as a mutagen by substituting for chemically related components of the DNA molecule and thus, disrupts a part of the genetic message. Some researchers hold the theory that caffeine itself may not be a mutagen in humans or other animals, but may still be a genetic threat by inhibiting natural repair or synthesis of DNA damaged by other chemical agents or by radiation.

Still others believe that one of the breakdown products of caffeine causes birth defects in animals. Since the breakdown products of caffeine vary from one species to another, findings in other species, they say, may not apply to humans.

Still another study points to the fact that pregnant women eliminate caffeine from their bodies at slower rates and this slowdown may have something to do with such pathologies. The study found that the prolongation in elimination of caffeine during pregnancy, particularly in later stages, returns to normal following delivery.[5]

Whatever the theory, however, the message is abundantly clear: *pregnant women should avoid coffee and all sources of caffeine.*

One of the most far-reaching of these warnings came from the FDA's *Drug Bulletin,* which is mailed to 967,000 health professionals, including 420,000 doctors, 200,000 nurses and 120,000 pharmacists.[6]

The government bulletin warned in language unmistakably clear: "... FDA advises that as a precautionary measure, pregnant and potentially pregnant women be advised to eliminate or limit their consumption of caffeine-containing products."

FDA went on to caution that cola syrup, often taken for morning sickness, contains caffeine. Many soft drinks, even those containing citrus flavors, may also contain added caffeine. And for this reason, the FDA warned, patients should be encouraged to *read the labels.* They also should talk to their physicians before taking any drug, including those available without a prescription. They should be advised to avoid caffeine-containing drugs in view of the ready availability of noncaffeine-containing alternatives. (See Chapter 11 for a list of drugs to avoid).

Still more support for a curb on caffeine use by pregnant women came from the executive director of CSPI, Michael Jacobson, Ph.D., in a four-page letter to physicians and other health professionals. Jacobson said: "We have carefully reviewed the scientific literature and concluded that the consumption of caffeine increases the risk of birth defects and other reproductive problems. We urge you to consider the evidence that implicates caffeine in reproductive problems. We hope you will counsel your patients who are pregnant or may become pregnant to avoid caffeine."

Thus the evidence is steadily mounting which overwhelmingly indicts coffee and its addictive agent, caffeine, for causing serious birth defects in our nation's children. Virtually all of the nation's major medical groups and health organizations support the belief that caffeine *could* cause birth defects, and to be on the safe side, pregnant women ought not to drink coffee at all.

Certainly, cautions such as these should not be taken lightly. The future of the nation may well depend on it.

Caffeine And The Pill

Oral contraceptives may provide still another arena for debate, and yet another shred of damning evidence against coffee.

Many studies have shown that males and females can and do metabolize some drugs differently. It has also been shown that oral contraceptives can decrease the metabolism of some drugs. Thus, it might be a fair question to ask: can oral contraceptives modify the way caffeine is metabolized, to the direct detriment of females?

The answer: they do.

A study undertaken by researchers in Nashville, Tenn. heightens the concern of pregnant women, and perhaps of all women, who take contraceptives.

The study revealed that females who take oral contraceptives have an impaired elimination capacity for caffeine. The effect was noted not only in women who drank higher levels of coffee, but also those who drank as little as two-to-four cups per day.

Given this to be the case, it might be suggested that caffeine may have a more severe effect on women taking oral contraceptives because of the longer period of time it takes to eliminate this drug.

The bottom line of their research was that with long-term caffeine use, accumulation of caffeine may occur in such individuals and, the report concluded, "it would be reasonable therefore to recommend that women taking OCS (oral contraceptive steroid) and pregnant mothers should moderate their intake of caffeine."

Bodies That Speak

Several times in this book, you'll hear me suggest that when your body hurts, it's trying to tell you something. And the bodies of women often have something important to say during the cycles of life.

Many respondents in our study reported that they began to vehemently dislike coffee when they approached their menstrual period or became pregnant. Because of some inexplicable hormonal change, drinking coffee for these women became entirely unappetizing. While we have found no formal research to explain this phenomena, it was repeated often enough to suggest a basis for concern.

Somehow, the bodies of these women began rejecting coffee and caffeine. It was as if their bodies *knew* that coffee presents a serious threat to the unborn and sought to announce that fact to a naive and unknowing mother.

It's my belief that these women—and the rest of us—should become wary of these telltales of future danger. We should listen to our bodies. They tell us the truth: Coffee is dangerous to our health.

Is Seeing Believing?

It has been 17 years since the U.S. Surgeon General issued his famous report linking cigarette smoking with cancer, heart disease, and a wide variety of pathological phenomena.

In 1964, there were approximately 53 million people who smoked. Since then, some 30 million have given up smoking. But more importantly, because of population increases, more than 54 million Americans still smoke!

Can you imagine that. Thousands of studies have implicated cigarette smoking in higher death rates and still millions of

Americans smoke. How can this be? They either don't believe, or don't care that they will be stricken with any one of a half-dozen forms of cancer, several types of heart disease and stroke, or a plethora of other medical ailments, just by smoking cigarettes. They just don't believe!

The Disbelievers

I'm really not surprised. I think many people can carry their disbeliefs about pathological cause and effect to its ultimate, and deadly conclusions. They have to test for themselves whether the relationship is true or false, and more importantly, they must determine if it holds true for themselves.

For example, it has been proven—beyond a shadow of a doubt—that cigarette smoking will shorten your life by many years—through cancer, through heart disease, and through any number of other ailments.[8]

And still millions disbelieve. Even when confronted, face-to-face, with overwhelming evidence.

At the University of Minnesota, hundreds of men and women participated in a voluntary research project which sought to determine whether high-risk heart attack patients would, or even could, mend their life styles and lower their risks.

All of the participants smoked cigarettes, were overweight and had seriously high cholesterol levels. All were prime candidates for heart attacks. Their program consisted of weekly meetings, dietary and weight reduction counseling, quit-smoking programs, and other informational seminars.

The results made a believer out of me—a believer in Man's fallibility, and in his inability to recognize the Grim Reaper's calling card.

The awful truth is that some participants took the program to heart and improved their medical outlook by changing their life styles. Others did not—and they died. "It just can't happen to me," they must have said to themselves—even to their dying breath.

Fibrocystic Breast Tumors: A Price For Disbelieving

The same question might be asked about coffee and caffeine consumption. A number of studies have implicated coffee consumption in the development of fibrocystic breast tumors among women. But in true form, doctors and researchers are still waging a rhetorical war about whether that proposition is true.

Whom do you believe? Well, when it comes to breast tumors, the *true believers* are the victims of this potentially dangerous condition who have eliminated the problem—by giving up the coffee habit.

What Is It?

Benign fibrocystic disease of the breast is a common clinical problem confronting American women. Physicians recognize the disease as a benign, self-limited process that usually, but not always, comes and goes around the menstrual period. Often the disease becomes relatively stable resulting in painful, firm, nodular breast tissue which can and easily does camouflage malignancy.

Not only can this condition mislead physicians (or lay persons) into dismissing malignant tissue as benign, but the condition itself is associated with a higher incidence of cancerous tissues.[9]

If the lumps are malignant, they must be removed—a costly, painful, and disfiguring operation—to prevent the spread of cancerous cells.[10]

Mammography has been helpful with early diagnosis of malignancy, but it can also, according to one researcher, be inaccurate. Therefore, women with chronic fibrocystic conditions may decline repeated mammographic examinations because of the well-publicized risk of radiation-induced cancer.

And here's where women are faced with a tough dilemma: repeated mammographic examinations may expose them to unnecessary cancer risks; foregoing such an examination may unnecessarily allow a malignant condition to go undetected. Biopsies can be painful and expensive.

The true role of coffee, then, becomes extraordinarily important for women. The available research suggests that reduced caffeine consumption can diminish or eliminate this breast disease.

In one of the pioneering studies on caffeine and fibrocystic breast disease by Dr. John P. Minton,[9] a group of 47 women with clinical fibrocystic disease of the breast were instructed to stop all methylxanthine caffeine consumption. Of the 47 women, 20 actually quit using coffee. These women averaged from four to nine cups of coffee per day (about 190 mg). The study showed that 13 experienced complete disappearance of all palpable breast nodules and other symptoms within one to six months. Only one of the 27 who continued her caffeine consumption experienced resolution of the disease.

Not only did the fibrocystic disease disappear in the majority of women who stopped drinking coffee, the need for diagnostic breast biopsies dropped more than *one-third*. That is, 26 of 27 women (96%), of the women who *did not* quit coffee drinking were required to undergo breast biopsies because their tumors had not disappeared whereas 7 of 20 (35%) of the women whose tumors disappeared following coffee cessation required biopsies.

Long-term followup of these women showed a continued resolution of breast symptoms as long as coffee abstinence was continued. *The breast disease returned, however, as soon as coffee drinking was resumed.*

The study also noted that smoking cigarettes tends to slow or prevent resolution in some patients and a complete resolution of the disease required a year or more in women 45 years and older. And as I indicated earlier, coffee drinkers are *more likely* to be cigarette smokers.

This study also noted that other previous studies tended to support their hypothesis. For example, in a matched study in Utah, Mormons exhibited significantly lower incidences of most types of cancers, including breast cancer, than did non-Mormons. The Mormon faith forbids coffee consumption. A similar study of

Seventh Day Adventists who hold a similar tenet, yielded similar results.

Other studies revealed results which confirm the prognosis: caffeine is not only linked with fibrocystic breast disease, but perhaps with breast cancer itself.

In our study, a significant number of women quit drinking coffee because they believed the fibrocystic breast disease they were experiencing was *caused* by their coffee consumption. About 10 percent of our sample had fibrocystic breast tumors. In *all instances,* the disease disappeared or had been significantly reduced following caffeine abstinence. Think of it! A complete 100 percent experienced remission. No more biopsies. No more nagging fears about malignancies. No more unnecessary risks. All this by hanging up the coffee cup.

The Center for Science in the Public Interest has long been aware of this special risk for women and has been one of the leaders in urging the FDA to require warning labels on caffeine-containing products to alert women about caffeine's potential harmful effects. According to the CSPI, physicians are generally not too concerned about alleviating the pain and lumps which accompany fibrocystic disease. The *Merck Manual,* a standard physician's handbook states that "treatment of fibrocystic disease is rarely required."

But CSPI noted that the controversy over fibrocystic lumps and coffee consumption is far from over. They noted that several breast experts refused to accept Minton's findings because Minton did not define "fibrocystic breast disease."

Dr. Darrow Haagensen, assistant professor of experimental surgery at Duke University, was one who questioned the findings. Haagensen, according to CSPI, claims that there are three distinctly different breast disorders which have all been classified as "fibrocystic breast disease."

Fifty percent of all women experience cyclical problems—including both breast lumps and pain—before menstruation. Second, many women have "diffusely lumpy breasts;" these lumps do not diminish after menstruation. Neither do the "discrete masses" associated with a third type of breast disorder. Within this category of breast disorders are gross cystic disease, the most common benign breast lesion (afflicting 7 percent of all women), and fibroadenoma (afflicting 5 percent of all women). Women with gross cystic disease, according to Haagensen, have a two to five times greater chance of developing breast cancer than women who have never had the fibrocystic disease.

Another doctor, Dr. Gordon Schwartz, professor of surgery at the Jefferson Medical College in Philadelphia and medical director of the Breast Health Foundation, also criticized Minton for not distinguishing between the several types of breast disorders. Schwartz says that cyclical breast lumps and pain are the only type of breast disorders which he believes can be diminished with coffee abstinence.

According to the CSPI, however, Minton claims that his studies were performed on women with "persistent unrelenting breast lumps and pain," not associated with the hormonal changes accompanying menstruation. He noted that some women whom he treated had fluid-filled cysts, a manifestation of gross cystic disease.

Our informal research revealed much the same results as Minton's. When coffee consumption was discontinued, the breast lumps disappeared—whether they were cyclical or not. And none of these women could be convinced that their problems were associated with anything but coffee.

Rose Kushner, executive director of the Breast Cancer Advisory Center and a member of the President's National Cancer Advisory Board, believes Minton's findings will reduce the number of biopsies.

"Doctors take out every lump and bump so they won't be hit with malpractice suits," she claimed. "With Minton's new findings," she said, "doctors will oftentimes have an alternative to biopsy, and thus, both help keep down health costs and save women from the trauma of breast biopsy."

Kushner also believes Minton's therapy is valuable because of the physical relief it might bring. "There is no reason," she asserted, "for women to have excruciating pain."[11]

So the controversy among the "experts" continues. And all the while, the suffering multitudes will seek their own self-counsel and kick the coffee habit. Research which will verify Minton's work may take years to finish and the American Cancer Society vows they will not inform the public about Minton's findings until other scientists have verified his work.

Will you be waiting, watching and wondering too? Or will you join the believers and kick the coffee habit?

10

Kids Are Junkies Too

There are 15,000,000 adults in this country who chronically abuse coffee and caffeine to such a degree that they're rightfully called, "coffee addicts." Worse yet, there are millions of kids who are junkies too. Their drug, however, is caffeine—the caffeine which was originally purged from coffee and added to soft drinks by manufacturers. The commercials and ads encourage your children to gulp down these sodas. In record numbers, manufacturers are fattening their profits. Good for them ... not good for us.

According to beverage industry sources, Americans consume an average of 33.6 gallons of soft drinks each year. The average consumption of coffee, by the way, is 27.8 gallons per person each year. And milk, touted as nature's most perfect food, trails the junk juices with consumption put at 24.8 gallons per year.

That means that Americans drink about one can of soft drink per day, *every day*. But wait. Not all Americans drink soft drinks. The soft drink industry, unwilling to share any information about average consumption of soft drinks among those who actually drink them, keeps those figures shrouded in secrecy. Obviously, though, it's a safe bet that people who *do* consume soft drinks down a *great* deal more than just a can a day. Some are drinking it at levels which can produce caffeinism and caffeine addiction— 5, 10, 15, even 20 cans or bottles a day.

There is no way to determine just exactly how many soft drink caffeine addicts we have in this country, but I can guarantee, it would really blow your mind. And millions of them, no doubt, are kids.

The soft drink business is a $12-billion-a-year industry and it's growing at a rate of about three percent to four percent a year. The king of the soft drink business is colas—colas dripping with caffeine.

In the U.S., Coke and Pepsi have for years commanded close to two-thirds of the market. Dozens of other less hazardous flavors fight for the rest of the business.

Coca-Cola now controls about 34 percent of the soft drink market; PepsiCo holds down 24 percent; and Dr Pepper earns about 7 percent of the market.[1] As you can see, the non-caffeinated beverages find it tough going in the soft drink marketplace. Royal Crown, which has been trying to capitalize on America's growing concern about caffeine consumption, is finding that penetrating the market with its healthier non-caffeinated cola is more than difficult. Making headway against the caffeinated cola giants is almost impossible.

What Goes Into Your Colas

Just try to find out what's in the colas your children are drinking these days and you'll find it a frustrating business. Sure, some soft drink manufacturers list the ingredients on the bottle or can, but try and find out how much caffeine is in "The Real Thing." Coca-Cola doesn't tell you and it never has. Neither does Pepsi-Cola.

The FDA says that caffeine is named as a *necessary* ingredient in the official definition of a cola drink. But once the standard has been developed, the manufacturer is exempt from telling you exactly how much of what is inside.

Thus, you have no way to determine whether Coke or Pepsi is a wholesome drink suitable for young children. As a matter of fact, it could be as suitable as giving your child a can of beer, a cup of coffee or a pack of cigarettes.

Soft drinks are almost all sugar, water, artificial flavorings and colorings, plus teeth-rotting phosphoric acid. But who knows for sure? The manufacturers are keeping the ingredients "trade secrets," they say. And we say if we knew, we would be better able to judge the potential health hazards the beverages represent. As it is, we know fully well that there are millions of caffeinated soft drink addicts in the country, as well as coffee addicts. No one has yet documented the proportions of the soft drink addict problem, but it's likely to be a massive one. And more importantly, it's likely to include millions of our children, whose developing minds and bodies are being damaged by these caffeine-laden drinks—damaged in ways which we shudder to think of but can only guess.

Why Colas Are Especially Dangerous For Kids

Caffeine's effects depend on both dose and body weight. The less you weigh, the greater the effect. Hence, women generally are more greatly affected than men, and children are more greatly affected than adults.

For example, a kid who drinks a Coke or a Dr Pepper may experience the same harmful caffeine effect as an adult who drinks *four* cups of coffee.[2] And four cups of coffee, in turn, is sufficient to touch off the start of *any* of the ailments this book discusses. It's nearly double the daily caffeine intake regarded by doctors as "safe."

There is ample evidence that all of the disturbances which adults experience through caffeinated coffee can also occur to children who imbibe excessive amounts of caffeinated beverages.

The amount of caffeine contained in several cans of cola can cause sleeplessness and jumpiness in children. In one study, researchers have shown that even small amounts of caffeine caused nervousness and increased motor activity.

Your kids, who appear otherwise healthy, may complain of such symptoms as rapid heartbeat or insomnia. They may be drinking excessive amounts of cola beverages.[3]

Into the Mouths of Babes

The problem of caffeinism is limited not only to children and adolescents. Infants are most assuredly affected too.

Fetuses, as we have shown, are subjected to caffeine incursions into their developing minds and bodies in an amount equal to that of the mother. Once born, they can continue to receive unhealthy doses of caffeine through their mother's milk. Several nursing mothers in our survey reported that their babies spent wakeful, restless nights because of, in all likelihood, *their* caffeine intake.

Another report told of a mother who found that her two-month-old twins started sleeping through the night immediately after she stopped drinking eight glasses of iced tea each day.

As if parents didn't have enough problems with their children they allow caffeine to create new ones. One study showed that about 18 percent of infants under two years consumed some caffeine. In the six-to-eleven-month group, infants who consumed caffeine received a mind-bending 77 mg per day. This is equivalent to about 19 ounces of cola.

Given these extremely high levels of consumption by infants so young, it's not surprising that we have mothers who complain of colicky children.

The infant who keeps his mother and father awake nightly is almost legendary. Adolescents who "can't sit still" in school and give daylong performances as classroom flibbertigibbets are as common as recess and multiplication tables. Just ask any teacher. And the *cause* of the problem may be just as common: Too Much Caffeine.

The warning should be amply clear: infants and adolescents should not be given caffeinated beverages. And consumption of these beverages by older children should be monitored carefully and kept at minimum levels or eliminated entirely.

11

Are You Hooked On Coffee?

The immediate concern of all people who read this book is likely to be, and indeed ought to be, "Am I hooked?"

The answer to that question is simple—only *you* can tell. How? We'll give you some guidelines.

Being hooked on coffee is not necessarily a simple numbers game. Drinking four to six cups of coffee a day, or even eight cups a day, does not *automatically* mean you're a coffee addict. Nor are you *automatically* exonerated if you're drinking only a cup or two of coffee. The key question to ask yourself is whether or not coffee has become a "harmful dependence" for you, regardless of the *amount* you drink. Is coffee causing physical or psycholgical disturbances to your health? Do you *depend* on coffee daily in order to gain some sense of physical well-being?

If you answer no to both, chances are coffee is not causing you problems—you can take it or leave it as you like. If you answer yes to either of the questions, you may well have a problem. And if you answer yes to both—you are definitely addicted to coffee. To help you decide for sure, let's first talk about your coffee habit:

your consumption, your coffee-related health problems, your dependence.

The Caffeine Danger Point

One of the first steps to help you decide whether or not you're chemically dependent on coffee is to measure your coffee intake. Just how much coffee—and caffeine—are you ingesting each day? Higher levels *suggest* such a dependence, but in no case do they *prove* it.

Various researchers have used values ranging from 200 mg to 750 mg of caffeine per day as a presumed "danger point" above which you are likely to suffer from caffeinism[1] or what we'll call caffeine overdose.

Pharmacologists consider doses of caffeine which exceed 250 mg as "large". And while caffeine is extremely variable in its effect on different people, 250 mg is described by many researchers as the "critical point" which separates safe from excessive use, and perhaps, accepted versus addictive use.

To put it another way, two to three cups of coffee per day is about what most folks can safely tolerate. Above that amount, you're ingesting too much coffee, and if your coffee contains caffeine, you're also ingesting too much caffeine.

In a 1969 study by Drs. Avram Goldstein and Sophia Kaiser at the Stanford University School of Medicine, it was found that it takes five or more cups of coffee a day to create a physical dependency in most people. That means that more than 30,000,000 people are in medical trouble. These millions drink five or more cups of coffee per day, or *double* the medically accepted guidelines. And that's coffee alone. They consume substantial additional amounts of caffeine in the other beverages they drink as well.

When all sources are considered, one study concluded, a conservative estimate is that 30,000,000 to 50,000,000 adult Americans function with a daily caffeine intake of more than 500-600 milligrams per day. As many as 10 percent of Americans, some 15,000,000 people, consume more than 1,000 mg of caffeine per day—three to four times the amount considered "dangerous" to your health and most assuredly an addictive level.

These numbers truly suggest that America is on a drug binge of truly epidemic proportions and most of the victims don't even know it.

What's Your Caffeine Consumption?

Getting a precise measurement of your caffeine consumption is about as easy as estimating the number of noodles in a bowl of soup. Not only do noodle counts change from bowl to bowl, but even the bowl itself is apt to be variable in size, making standardizing measures an impossible effort. Yet it is crucial to determine how much caffeine poisons your system daily.

Our research and that of most others we've uncovered suggests that people tend to minimize their coffee and caffeine consumption. We would expect that many coffee drinkers are vaguely aware of the hazards excessive coffee drinking presents, and thus, tend to underinflate their consumption in an effort to rationalize the poor treatment of their bodies.

But even if they were honestly trying to keep such records, the task would be quite impossible without several better guidelines.

Good To The Last

Consider for a moment, the imprecise measurement called "the cup."

There are an exceedingly wide variety of coffee cups and mugs on the commercial and institutional market these days, varying considerably in their capacities.

The dainty little demitasse cup served at formal dinner tables is likely to contain about five ounces of coffee, maybe less. Hardier coffee drinkers, when left to their own less formal devices, usually opt for a somewhat larger cup because it helps eliminate needless trips to the coffeepot. The fairly common household mug holds about eight ounces. And there are many super mugs on the market, as much for novelty as for coffee freaks. These mugs hold anywhere from 10 to 15, even 20 ounces of brew.

Which do *you* use? Chances are, you may use several sizes. You may start the day with your favorite coffee mug at home, probably an eight-ouncer. You may switch to a larger or smaller cup at work. At the restaurant where you have lunch, you'll get something else. And when you're out to dinner at a friend's house, you'll find something different yet.

Obviously, the only way to overcome the difficulties inherent in this problem is to get a better understanding not as to how many *cups* of coffee you drink . . . but how many *ounces* of coffee you drink. We figure that most folks use an eight-ounce cup which contains probably six to seven ounces of coffee. Coffee commercials notwithstanding, *nobody* fills a cup to the "brim."

There are two more variables which serve to confuse the issue further. One is the *method* you choose to prepare your coffee or tea, and the second is the length of *time* you allow the coffee or tea to brew.

Research has revealed that personal preferences greatly affect the amount of caffeine available in the coffee or tea you drink. In fact, coffee prepared by the dripolator method in one study had *twice* the caffeine of instant coffee. This study also noted that it is possible for a cup of *tea* brewed five minutes to be equal in caffeine content to a cup of instant coffee or a can of cola.[2] So much for the notion that tea always has less caffeine than coffee.

The table on the next page will illustrate the problem.

The research suggest that brewing time extracts more caffeine from coffee and tea. The results show that increases of just five minutes in brewing time can increase the potential caffeine in your coffee cup by anywhere from 3 to 14 percent.

Coffee prepared by a dripolator method contained, on the average, about 128 percent more caffeine that the instant-freeze-

Table 6. Caffeine content in coffee by brand, type, and method of preparation.

Brand	Instant freeze-dried	percolator non-automatic 5 min.	10 min.	percolator automatic	dripolator non-automatic	dripolator automatic
		mg./per cup				
A	61	97	105	93		
B		112	116	107	137	153
C	69					
D		110	125	120		
E	68					
F	63	108	120	97	146	150
G	70					
Mean of all brands per cup	66	107	118	104	142	151

Source: Adapted from results compiled by Bunker and McWilliams, *Caffeine Content of Common Beverages*, Journal of the American Dietetic Assn., Jan. 1979.

dried coffee brands. It makes a great deal of difference, then, what sort of coffee you're pouring into your system.

But let's find out exactly what you are using your body as the dumping ground for. Just how much caffeine is adulterating your system?

To ease your computation and solidify the variables, we've prepared a chart which, in short work, will tell you the awful truth. Chances are, you're drinking a lot more coffee—and caffeine—than you ever thought possible.

Coffee Quiz

To find out, first determine what kind of coffee you use and how you prepare it. Using table 6, determine the *average* caffeine level of coffee the way *you* prepare it. Then, multiply the number of milligrams of caffeine per ounce times the number of ounces you drink each day. Remember that most coffee drinkers are using an eight-ounce cup, but to be sure, measure yours.

Coffee Method	Average Mg Per Oz.	Total Oz. You Drink	Your Total Caffeine
Instant	13.2	_____	_____
Automatic Percolator	20.8	_____	_____
Non-Automatic Percolator	21.4	_____	_____
Automatic Dripolator	28.4	_____	_____
Non-Automatic Dripolator	30.2	_____	_____
		Total Mg Caffeine:	_____

Other Caffeine Sources

Fortunately, the known caffeine content of the various soft drinks and over-the-counter drugs is reasonably constant and reliable. Therefore, it's easy to compute. Just scan the list below and calculate how much poison you're drinking.

Table 7. Caffeine content of selected carbonated beverages.

Beverage	Caffeine Per Ounce	Your Caffeine Total
Coca Cola	5.39	————
Dr Pepper	5.08	————
Mountain Dew	4.58	————
Diet Dr Pepper	4.51	————
TAB	3.75	————
Pepsi-Cola	3.50	————
RC Cola	3.00	————
Diet RC	2.75	————
Diet-Rite	2.64	————

As you can see from the figures, it's fairly easy to eclipse the caffeine danger point with soft drinks *alone.* Have a couple of Cokes and you've already injected yourself with 130 mg of caffeine. If you're young son or daughter is the one doing the drinking (and he or she probably is), you can just about double the caffeine effect. It's enough to blow your mind (and his as well). If you're drinking *both* coffee and caffeinated soft drinks, your daily caffeine levels could be reaching stellar proportion, too.

The Drugs You Take

Remember that many of the drugs you may be taking also contain caffeine. Aspirin and other analgesics do. So do stay-awake remedies and thousands of prescription and non-prescription drugs. If you're taking some of these, beware. You could be doubling, tripling, and even quadrupling your caffeine consumption levels.

And many caffeine users are doing just that. Some days their caffeine usages reaches mind boggling levels while on others, it may be lower, but still dangerous to health. To plot your highs and lows during a weekly level, fill in the work pages in the Appendix at the end of this book. I'm sure you're in for a big (and unwelcome) surprise.

Table 8. Caffeine content of selected over-the-counter drugs.

Anacin	32
Aqua-ban	100
Caffedrine	200
Cenegistic	15
Cope	32
Coryban-D	30
Dristan Decongestant	16
Empirin	32
Excedrin	65
Goody's Headache Powders	33
Midol	32
No Doz	100
Neo-Synephrine	15
Sinapils	32
Triaminicin	30
Vanquish	33
Vivarin	200

Source: U.S. Department of Health and Human Services. Public Health Service. HHS Publication No. (FDA) 81-1081

Table 9. Caffeine content of selected prescription drugs.

Apectol	40
Cafergot	100
Darvon	32
Esgic	40
Fiorinal	40
Migral Tablets	50
Migralam Capsules	100
Soma Compound	32

Source: U.S. Department of Health and Human Services. Public Health Service. HHS Publication No. (FDA) 18-1081.

The Final Tally

Now estimate your caffeine consumption. How do you rank against the medically-accepted standards? Are you just average? Are you a caffeine junkie?

Daily Caffeine From Coffee	_____
Daily Caffeine From Soft Drinks	_____
Daily Caffeine From Other Sources	_____
Total Daily Caffeine:	_____

If you're like most coffee drinkers, you'll find that not only are you drinking a good deal more *coffee* than you at first might have believed, you also are ingesting significantly excessive levels of *caffeine*—both at great risk to your health and well-being.

Millions of Americans are well past the danger point and are, as the numbers suggest, addicted to coffee. The addiction may perhaps be inferred by the excessive consumption, and therefore, the excessive tolerance.

Tolerance, as we indicated earlier, is one of the variables which can be used to determine caffeine addiction. It's a simple fact that for millions of coffee drinkers, one or two cups is simply not enough. They have to have more and more coffee to obtain the feeling of well-being they seek. Their bodies grow more and more tolerant to these higher levels.

It's the same stuff which thousand-dollar-a-week drug addictions and pack-and-a-half cigarette smokers are made.

Without these higher levels of drug intake, the addict begins to suffer from withdrawal and other discomforting symptoms. That discomfort, in turn, helps perpetuate the habit because the addict seeks relief from distress by ingesting more drugs.

Eventually, for chronic users, daily doses exceeding nine cups of coffee per day may seem routine. Such tolerance and habituation almost certainly develop when the substance is so chronically abused.

That's why I tend to dismiss the arguments of those who claim that if you drank 15 to 20 cups of *anything,* you might well suffer adverse effects. That proposition, although patently untrue—is also academic. What is more relevant to our hypothesis is that it is a medical rarity for anyone to daily drink 25 cups of hot chocolate, or 25 cups of milk, or 25 cups of orange juice or apple cider. But millions and millions of Americans are drinking coffee at these unhealthy levels *because of its addictive qualities,* and not because of any intrinsic physiological or nutritive value. The fact is they're *hooked* on coffee in a way that *only occurs* with addictive drugs. And that's why it's dangerous.

Coffee's Harmful Effects

Millions and millions of Americans are reaching a rather personal understanding of the harmful effects of coffee drinking. The professional literature on the subject is replete with case histories of men and women whose bodies and minds have been pained and crippled by their coffee consumption. In our own research, we've uncovered hundreds of coffee drinkers who, through their own experimentation, became aware that coffee was ruining their lives and decided to quit. Thousands of Americans are making that discovery each day and make the break for caffeine freedom. But millions more aren't sure. They are not absolutely certain what bitter prognosis the coffee reaper brings. Research is not altogether certain of the *exact* role that coffee and caffeine plays in the pathologies. And their own bodies are not crying out with ailments seeking immediate relief. In short, they are unmoved by the testimony, either from within or without.

It is here that we're going to get into some admittedly circular reasoning which can be clarified more by experiment than by rhetoric.

Coffee drinkers have a wide range of tolerance for both coffee and caffeine. Many people can drink 10 or 20 cups of coffee a day without overt complaint. Others drink only a cup or two a day and experience throbbing headaches and tremulousness.

So where's the real danger point? It is at whatever point coffee and caffeine starts doing something which is harmful either to your mind or body—regardless of whether or not you are aware of it. Many of the medical risks of coffee drinking may become manifest to you later in life. Others can be made startling clear right now—just by quitting.

That's right. Just forget the rationalizations, the excuses, and quit. Simple, right? Well, maybe not.

I can already hear you saying, "I can quit anytime I want, I just don't want to quit right now," or, "Why would I want to do that? Coffee isn't doing *me* any harm." I have heard these excuses many times before. I've heard it from practicing alcoholics, I've heard it from drug addicts, I've heard it from men and women hooked on cigarettes. And it's just baloney.

If you're not hooked, all you have to do is quit drinking coffee and that's that. If you are hooked, you'll begin inventing all sorts of excuses and never "get around" to quitting.

If you can quit without complaint, without remorse, if you truly can "take it or leave it," the chances are that regardless of the coffee you drink, you may not be addicted (which isn't to stay it isn't damaging your body). But wait, there's more.

If you can quit without experiencing withdrawal symptoms, you're probably not suffering from caffeinism. We've talked with many men and women who drank anywhere from 2 to 25 cups per day and *did not* experience withdrawal. Everybody is different. And so are you.

If, after going without coffee for two or three weeks and you can honestly say you don't feel any better, chances are coffee was not significantly affecting your mind and your body.

Is that likely? Not a chance. *None* of the 200 former coffee drinkers in our research was able to make that statement. Every last former coffee drinker we interviewed mentioned at least two or three ways in which they felt better after giving up coffee.

Some of their stories were quite remarkable and we'll be reporting their stories more fully in the next chapter. The method is absolutely foolproof. If our research is suggestive of possible results, anywhere from 15,000,000 to 50,000,000 coffee drinkers could be feeling a thousand percent better in just two short weeks if they'd only kick the coffee habit. It may take at least two weeks—maybe more—to flush the coffee poisons from your system and to recover from any withdrawal you're likely to encounter upon quitting. But when you're done—you'll feel terrific.

Caffeine and Addictive Withdrawal

One of the attributes of addictive drugs, and caffeine has certainly demonstrated its membership to this elite club, is that they produce in its victims, periods of drug withdrawal. Those distressing physiological and mental effects accompany discontinuance of the drug.

In fact, one way to determine if you are indeed "hooked" on caffeine, to confirm what coffee and caffeine are doing to your mind and body, is to discontinue its use and chart the results.

Most moderate to heavy users of coffee report severe, throbbing headaches when they quit coffee, usually beginning within 18 to 24 hours after their last cup.

Since the headache is promptly relieved by more caffeine, the clinical link has been established. This "cause and effect" is so predictable that headaches are now universally cited as one of the symptoms of withdrawal and therefore caffeine addiction.

One researcher, in fact, believes that many individuals who claim they suffer from recurrent "tension headaches" may in fact be suffering from repeated episodes of caffeine withdrawal.

The same researcher noted that caffeine withdrawal headaches tend to occur on weekends, perhaps because work-related caffeine use dramatically reduces on Saturday and Sunday, traditional days off.

The headache typically begins with a feeling of cerebral fullness and progresses to a diffuse, painful throbbing.

Many respondents reported their headaches lasted for days, even weeks. Plain aspirin offered the sufferers little help. But, as you might expect, analgesics which also contain caffeine worked wonders on the withdrawal headaches, for the obvious reason.

Exercise and heavy work tend to aggravate the headache problems, as well as other withdrawal symptoms. Many of our respondents reported extreme drowsiness, a disinterest in their work. Others reported lightheadedness, an inability to concentrate, increased irritability, dizziness. Some reported getting terribly depressed for two and three weeks at a time; nausea, fever, chills, sweaty palms, weakness, uneasiness. Still others reported rhinorrhea (runny nose), nervousness and depression.

If many of these symptoms seem to suggest an ailment more severe than caffeine withdrawal, you are quite right, a fact one prominent researcher has also duly noted and expanded.

In Victorian England at the turn of the century, the typical coffee drinker was medically described as a person who was "tremulous, loses his self-command, is subject to fits of agitation and depression, and has a haggard appearance ... As with other agents, a renewed dose of the poison gives temporary relief, but at the cost of future misery."

Dr. John F. Greden, in a pioneering work on caffeinism, complained in the American Journal of Psychiatry, that although huge amounts of coffee are consumed annually, a review of pertinent literature failed to reveal any significant mention of caffeinism. Greden went on to say that a random review of 100 recent outpatient psychiatric records at his medical center failed to reveal a single listing of coffee- or tea-drinking patterns, despite the fact that 42 of these records referred to anxiety symptoms. These symptoms are not at all unlike those which caffeine and caffeine withdrawal can produce.

One wonders how may prescriptions for Valium and other tranquilizers have been handed out to patients who were suffering from undiagnosed caffeine addiction, an addiction which one researcher shows could affect as many as 15 percent of all Americans.

Finally, as a challenge to your system and a doublecheck on your caffeine addiction, you might try drinking a cup of coffee about two or three weeks after you've quit.

If you've been a coffee addict, a cup or two of coffee will send you on a trip like you'd never believe. The great majority of respondents in our research and that of others, report a marked deterioration in their well-being if they reintroduce caffeine into their systems. The situation is not unlike the cigarette addict who lights up a smoke after quitting for a month. He instantly gets nauseous and dizzy.

What this really tells you about is the potency of the drug involved. Is coffee and caffeine really that dangerous? Just try drinking again after you've quit. You'll be absolutely amazed what abuse you've been sending your body through. You'll wonder how on earth you continued to drink the dirty stuff. As one of our respondents put it, "the thought of drinking coffee now is really repulsive to me."

A Time To Act

The coffee drinking reader, then, must now face the bottom line and answer two important questions: (1) are you addicted to coffee?; (2) Is coffee causing you mental or physical injury?

Based on the testimony you've read, you ought to clearly see the light. If you are drinking three or more cups of coffee each day, the chances are overwhelming that coffee is doing you more harm than good. And it's just as true whether you are aware of the damage or not; or for that matter, whether the damage has become manifest or like heart disease or cancer, is lurking in some distant corner of your life.

Secondly, if you're drinking five or more cups a day, the chances are quite likely that you are *addicted* to coffee. That is, you depend on a harmful chemical to get you through the day. And because it robs you of your freedom to think and act as you choose, you're no better nor worse than any junkie.

The most important question is this: Can you accept the truth? Can you surrender to the facts?

If you can, take back your freedom right now! If you're still unsure, why not take the acid test? Learn the extent of your addiction and the degree of your pain and suffering by kicking the coffee habit. It's easy to do and I'll show you how.

12

The Great Coffee Break

The overwhelming preponderance of evidence, both historical and contemporary, suggests in no uncertain way that coffee drinking is dangerous to your health—particularly in amounts of three or more cups per day.

If you're drinking more—you're likely to be in for a load of trouble. But taken even in small amounts, as we have seen, coffee and caffeine can be injurious to your health.

Every year, millions of American coffee drinkers are getting wise to the great medical dangers posed by coffee drinking and they're striking out for healthier lives by kicking this addictive habit.

They've seen, firsthand, how coffee and caffeine addicts their bodies and minds; how it causes considerable pain and suffering and exposes them to an ever-widening specter of deadly diseases.

What's more, they're doing it largely on their own initiative. They're putting two and two together and have come up with "forget it." They no longer want any part of this liquid empty of nutrition but infested with danger. Even while medical, clinical and governmental institutions drag their collective feet on indicting the drug—these quitters have already made up their minds. And more power to them.

I spoke to nearly 200 of these quitters who told their stories in the most humane of words, with almost evangelistic fervor. They revealed how coffee was ruining their lives and sending their bodies down an endless gantlet of future medical dangers.

There was no need to convince these people that coffee and caffeine "might" have something to do with their multitudinous complaints: *they were absolutely positive.* No doctor, no report, no study could convince them more. And to a man and woman, none could ever conceive the possibility of returning to the drug—regardless of how some future study might somehow exonerate the drug of this or that symptom. Life was now, they said, simply too much of a healthy blessing to take the risk. Their experiences along this road to a healthier life are worth repeating.

How We Get Started

Although the statistics are rapidly shifting as fewer and fewer young people take up coffee drinking, the bulk of American coffee drinkers, and therefore quitters, are middle-aged.

Those in our survey ranged in age from 23 to 80 years of age, and had coffee drinking histories that began as little as one year ago to some that stretched into as many as 70 years of coffee drinking.

Most quitters, however, were in their 30s, or 40s, and had been drinking coffee for about 10 to 15 years.

Their reasons for drinking coffee were almost uniformly trivial. Perhaps that says a great deal about how we socialize our young people, and how addictive habits perpetuate themselves—even in the absence of recognizable benefits.

Typical of their responses, was this candid analysis by a 41-year-old teacher. "'In the beginning," she said, "I drank it because it was the thing to do. I acquired a taste for it. But later, I drank it out of habit, out of physical addiction."

Virtually all of the coffee drinkers who were interviewed voiced similar attitudes. "I drank coffee because it was there," said a 30-year-old social worker who had been drinking it for 15 years.

Millions of coffee drinkers, yourself included, drink this dangerous brew for the same superficial reasons. Take a listen to their reasons and see if you don't hear *yourself* talking:

> "It is a social thing," said a young housewife.
> "It's just a thing to do," a dietitian told us.
> "It's just a sign of growing up."
> "I drank it because everybody at work drinks coffee."
> "You don't go on break and not drink coffee."
> "I didn't really enjoy the taste. I thought it was just stupid."
> "I drank it because it was there."
> "I drank it because it gave me something to do."
> "It was a sociable thing to do."
> "I drank coffee because it was available."

These are certainly not the comments of nutrition-minded people who drank coffee to brighten their health or otherwise engender well-being. Nor do their comments seem inspired by epicurean delight or affection for this drink. Rather, these are the comments of people who continue their addictive coffee drinking habits in mindless repetition. It's a humdrum routine which will be modified only when the pain and suffering associated with drinking coffee outweighs the "pleasures" of drinking, however slight and fleeting they may be.

This is the history of most but not all of the addicts we interviewed. A few, of course, truly relished the taste, the smell, the aroma of coffee. Sure, they may have been enticed into drinking by peer pressure, but what really kept them coming back, cup after cup, was the *taste* and that "good feeling" coffee produced.

The case of coffee addiction is not unlike that of alcohol addiction. Many alcoholics take their first drink in response to social pressures to conform ... to "try it out." Regardless of their reasons for starting, however, alcohol delivers the promises the abuser expects: feelings of confidence, well-being, happiness, success, or whatever. It is only when the alcoholic discovers, often through the intervention of another, that the drug is no longer keeping its promises and is delivering instead, some terrible mental and physical problems, that hope for recovery can begin.

The coffee drinker is much the same. It is only when he or she discovers that coffee is bringing much more harm than the good of a pick-me-up or mental stimulant, that the coffee "break" becomes an alternative resolution. Millions of Americans reached that point this past year. And the number is likely to continue to grow, in ever-increasing numbers.

Of the nearly 20 reasons coffee drinkers reported for quitting, by far and away the most prevalent was to seek escape from the distressing disturbances of the central nervous system. These are the type of disorders that have proven, time and time again, to be caused by the caffeine in coffee and other beverages and food products. Nearly 4 in 10 coffee drinkers made the break for this reason. But there were other reasons.

Table 10. Reasons Coffee Addicts Gave For Quitting Coffee	
Central Nervous System Disorders	39%
Gastrointestinal Problems	37%
Admitted Addiction	19%
Fibrocystic Breast Tumors	15%
Cancer Scare	9%
General Ill Health	6%
Bladder Problems	5%
Heart Problems	5%
Better Nutrition	5%
Other	4%

Obviously, some respondents gave more than one reason for quitting. Most gave several. But whatever their reasons, each of our quitters had a strong commitment to breaking the coffee habit—and that's precisely what you'll need, if you're going to make the great coffee break.

Such a commitment is necesssary because you may be in for some tough times ahead and without a firm resolve, you may never make it.

Is Quitting Difficult?

Giving up the coffee habit is relatively easy to do—once a commitment has been made to strike out for a healthier life. Without that commitment, the sheer momentum of your coffee drinking past is likely to keep you drinking for years to come.

Most sources describe coffee as "mildly" addictive. About that I'd have to both agree and disagree. Certainly, most addicts are hooked on the drug to such a degree that it greatly interferes with their home life, their work life, or their phyiscal life. That's the same criteria, by the way, that you would use to check yourself on alcoholism. If the drug interferes with any of these three areas—and you continue to take the drug—brother, you're in trouble.

On the other hand, I'd have to agree that coffee, for the vast majority of coffee drinkers, can be given up without the sort of difficulties that both alcoholics and drug addicts experience. As a matter of fact, many coffee addicts are pleasantly surprised that they could do it so easily.

Most of our survey respondents suddenly reached a "bottom point" when they made up their minds to kick the habit. Something clicked in their minds, like the young woman who said she quit because "coffee drinking was just stupid."

"Cold turkey" was another phrase that appeared time and time again in our study, most often used by men who, like their female counterparts, experienced little or no difficulty after the first few days.

Naturally, there are millions of coffee drinkers who have tried to quit, and failed. Most assuredly, their experiences are a great deal different than most of our respondents. Only a few in our group reported that "it was hard to do at first," or that "it took a lot of willpower to do it." Less than three percent reported having such difficulty. Most had a troublesome day or two, or even a week, but then immediately began to enjoy a most amazing rejuvenation—one that they never thought possible.

Withdrawal

Probably nothing is more mysterious in the entire coffee drinking scenario than the great variance in withdrawal symptoms among coffee quitters.

Reactions are so varied they are difficult to quantify either by severity or even type of symptom. Predicting either measurement based on coffee intake is a useless, ineffective exercise because here again, reactions are so varied.

What can be said without equivocation is that everyone's experiences upon quitting coffee are different; some experience withdrawal; some do not. Some quitters experience extremely painful withdrawal. Others report symptoms which are relatively mild. And obviously, what is mild to some is painful to others.

A few generalizations might well be made, however, on our group of 200 respondents. Generally speaking, fewer men report they suffer from withdrawal than women. In our study, more than three-fourths of the men reported no withdrawal symptoms whatsoever. Those men that did not report withdrawal symptoms reported drinking anywhere from 1 to 15 cups per day, with the average consumption being six cups per day.

About 80 percent of the women in the survey reported they suffered from withdrawal symptoms in varying degrees. But what was more surprising was that women in this survey could drink a great deal of coffee and still not report withdrawal symptoms. Average coffee consumption among those women not reporting withdrawal average 8.5 cups per day. At least two of the respondents who did not report withdrawal said they were drinking between 25 and 40 cups of coffee per day!

Thus, the sort of problems you might expect are pretty difficult to predict. You may have withdrawal symptoms. You may not. The degree of withdrawal symptoms is equally difficult to predict.

The Coffee Hangover

The most universal symptom of withdrawal is the headache and it can really be a bummer.

"I got headaches for four days like I thought I was going to die," one male respondent reported. A 49-year-old woman who reported drinking 10 cups of coffee a day for eight years told me "it felt like the top of my head was being squeezed in a vice. And I was so depressed." A 48-year-old woman who had been drinking nine cups for some 30 years, said she experienced the worst headache she ever had in her life. "I was too sick to take anything," she said. "I just crawled in bed and just about passed out."

As a matter of fact, the headache is so much a part of the withdrawal syndrome that coffee addiction can at least in some measure be suggested by its presence following coffee abstinence.

Margaret's Headaches Provided The Clues

Such was the case of a 27-year-old payroll supervisor. She had been drinking 10-15 cups of coffee per day for some 10 years before she decided to quit and here's her story.

"When the weekend came around, my husband and I wouldn't normally drink coffee and I started getting such bad headaches. I could hardly even function, they were so bad. Finally, I put two and two together and found it was the lack of coffee that was making me feel so miserable, so I gave it up."

Another woman made the same discovery when visiting her in-laws who were regular decaffeinated coffee drinkers. On weekends when she would visit her in-laws, she would get "frightful headaches" and she came to the same conclusion, it was time to get rid of all caffeine.

Other Withdrawal Pains

In addition to headaches, there's a long list of other withdrawal symptoms which attack the novice coffee quitter, unfortunately coming at a time when he or she leasts needs them.

Among those universally reported maladies are lethargy, light-headedness, sleeplessness, nervousness, tremulousness, depression, severe upset stomach, excitability, dizziness, diarrhea, grouchiness and irritability, tenseness, nausea, fever and chills, weakness; all this plus what many report as a genuine *craving* for coffee.

There is very little you can do about withdrawal symptoms. Most of our respondents just suffered through them. A few tried aspirin with no relief whatsoever. Some tried analgesics which contained caffeine and they recovered almost instantly—at the risk of future misery. Your best bet is to plan in advance and if you suffer from withdrawal, you'll at least be in a position to minimize it.

Selecting Your "I Quit" Day

When you decide to quit drinking coffee, make it easy on yourself. Chances are, if you're like most of us, you drink less coffee on the weekends so why not plan your Quit Day for a weekend. Not only plan your quitting day for a weekend, but try to pick a weekend when you don't expect to be too busy. Exercise can aggravate any headache or other withdrawal symptom you may have so take it easy and lay low. Hopefully, on Monday when it's time to go back to work, you'll be over most of your withdrawal and you'll be more ready to handle the week without problem.

You'll already know what it's like to face the workday morning without your usual cup of coffee. You already will have experienced meals without coffee, a certain level of work with coffee. You no doubt will be several steps ahead of the game.

Cold Turkey or Taper?

Whether you quit on the weekend or during the week, you may wish to consider tapering off your consumption, rather than to undertake the abrupt and total withdrawal of coffee suggested by the term, "cold turkey."

If you decide to taper, you may wish to consider taking your coffee "half-caff," that is, a combination of regular and decaffeinated coffee. In this way, you could well avoid the headaches and other withdrawal symptoms that many quitters undergo when they knock off their drinking suddenly.

You may also want to switch to tea as another way to taper down. Chances are, you'll be getting less than half your normal caffeine intake.

With either of these tapering methods, you can safely cut back your consumption and probably avoid any withdrawal. On the other hand, most of the respondents in our survey preferred to kick the habit all at once—right now. Frankly, I prefer the cold turkey method because it provides a sharp line of demarcation, separating old and new behavior. But it's your body. You be the judge.

Nutritious Coffee Substitutes

It's also a nice idea to stock up on alternative drinks before you quit. Check out Chapter 14 for ideas. Because coffee has been so much a part of your life, you're likely to be left with a gaping hole in your drinking life that craves to be filled. And we've got some good suggestions to consider.

Are You Going to Miss Coffee?

Most coffee quitters report that they don't miss coffee once they've endured whatever withdrawal may accompany their cessation. About 90 percent said they don't miss it at all.

Only those who really enjoyed their coffee drinking had those certain moments when they truly craved for a hot cup of coffee.

Those moments came when you might expect—when they'd just finished a meal, or when they were out for dinner or socializing with friends.

The experience of many of our respondents was even more emphatic. "I have really turned off the stuff completely. I don't like it at all." Another summed up a feeling that was fairly common, "I really can't stand it anymore. It makes me sick."

Are you going to miss coffee? About 1 chance in 100!

Falling Off The Wagon

Once you have cleared your system of coffee and caffeine, there may come a time when you're tempted—just this once—to have a cup or two of coffee.

I have a little warning for you: don't.

Reintroducing caffeine into your system once you have given it up is just like a former cigarette smoker taking a drag on a smoke or an alcoholic getting back into the booze; it's awful.

But don't take my word for it. Listen to the experts.

Many former coffee drinkers experience the same problem when they "challenge" their system by reintroducing the drug. A 59-year-old man reported that when he drank coffee while out to dinner he got "really hyper, all hopped up," he said. The coffee also gave him diarrhea for several days.

A 39-year-old woman who builds architectural models said a half-cup of coffee would act as a "super stimulus" to her. "In fact," she said, "even a sip or two now and I'm off."

That such reactions are commonplace among coffee drinkers who quit is compelling testimony to the tolerance levels that coffee addicts build up. It also substantiates their coffee addiction, which for many was not apparent prior to their quitting.

What Your Friends Will Say

The newly-reformed coffee addict is likely to experience at least some taunting and ridicule from her coffee-drinking associates. That's as it should be because the same thing happens to recovering alcoholics and smokers who give up their deadly cigarettes. For some reason, practicing addicts seem to find a need to justify their continued drug use by belittling the health-saving activities of those who quit. This is not always the case, but our respondents certainly took note of a tendency to be classified as "odd balls" for declining coffee on social occasions, and as "health nuts" because they wanted to improve their lives.

A 30-year-old bus driver told me that people "look at me kind of weird" when I say I don't want coffee. When they offer me a cup," he said, "I say 'no thank you.' But I always feel obligated to tell them I've quit."

A 36-year-old housewife agreed, saying "people always look at you funny, when you don't drink coffee."

Perhaps at least some of the discomfort these people are feeling is not because others are, in fact, treating them in ways which are particularly different. It may be because the quitters are themselves self-conscious.

"People thought I was crazy to quit coffee," a 30-year-old secretary said, "Americans are so geared to drinking coffee."

Another told me that "people try so hard to please you that it gets embarrassing. And you appear to be so difficult to please when all you really want is a glass of water. The hostess just doesn't feel like she's doing enough."

"Now I know what it's like to be an alcoholic at a cocktail party," another confided.

Although there may be a certain amount of testing or mild disapproval, the growing weight is on the side of the quitters. More and more people are kicking the coffee habit and opting for nutritious drinks that provide energy and healthful vitamins and minerals.

The same thing has happened among former cigarette smokers who used to be in distinct minority. Their numbers have swelled, however, and giving up cigarettes is now more "in" than ever.

A 28-year-old housewife probably said it best, "When I first stopped drinking I felt a little embarrassed. But in the last year I've noticed that a lot more people don't drink coffee so I don't feel bad. Non-coffee drinking seems to be more accepted now than when I first quit."

How You're Going To Feel

One of the most exciting discoveries you're likely to make when you quit drinking coffee is how great it really feels without it.

Coffee permeates a great many facets of your health and social well-being—and once your natural self has been reborn, it's easy to see what you've been missing.

Take the matter of sleep, for example. Dozens of men and women in our survey reported that once they had quit coffee, they began to be blessed with the most refreshing, deep sleep that they ever experienced. These reports came from people who previously had no complaints whatsoever about their sleep. In other words, they never *really knew* what a good night's rest was—until they had kicked the coffee habit.

The same is true for your general well-being. Many people told me they perceived themselves as calm, rational, easygoing types—*until* they quit coffee. Then they found out that they had been living a continual nightmare of mood swings, irritability, and jumpiness while drinking coffee. The problem behavior became known to them only *after* they had kicked the habit. That's one of the reasons why coffee is such an insidious drug. It works a heavy number on people—and the victims don't know it.

Coffee and Your Doctor

Perhaps the sorriest state of affairs in this whole coffee drinking controversy is the role which doctors fail to play at providing an essential link between the research community and the patient. To say that our nation's physicians are fulfilling this role adequately is an overstatement of the worst sort. It's not only untrue, it's dangerous to suggest that they do.

Table 11. Percent of persons 20 years of age and over who had been advised to change coffee habits. By daily consumption. United States, 1976

		Daily coffee consumption		
Advised to change coffee habits	All amounts	5 or more cups	Some, but less than 5 cups	Does not drink coffee
		Number		
Number of persons[1]	126,429	22,576	78,441	25,412
		Percent distribution		
Told to cut down on coffee				
Total	100.0	100.0	100.0	100.0
Yes	8.8	14.6	7.8	6.6
No	90.2	85.2	91.9	89.8
Unknown	1.0	0.3	0.3	3.6
Use decaffeinated coffee[2]				
Total		100.0	100.0	
Yes		10.5	9.1	
No		89.1	90.3	
Unknown		0.4	0.6	

[1]Excludes persons with unknown amount of daily coffee consumption.
[2]Doctor's advice to use decaffeinated coffee was not asked of those who did not drink coffee.

Source: Compiled by National Center for Health Statistics. U.S. Department of Health, Education, and Welfare.

It's sad to know that doctors only infrequently question their patients about their coffee consumption and patients perhaps just as often "withhold" that data from their doctors.

But for whatever reasons, the net effect is to have millions of patients endure pain and suffering and neither doctor nor patient know that coffee consumption is the cause of their complaints.

Listen to a 37-year-old office worker: "I was having real, real severe headaches, I mean, really bad. I would wake up with them every morning. And I went to a neurologist. And he called me up on the phone and told me to get in the hospital immediately. I think you have a brain tumor. I went in and I had an angiogram and it didn't turn up a thing. Finally, after I had been through psychological testing, all those physical tests, did they ask about my diet. I brought up the fact that I drank a lot of coffee and wondered how that was affecting me. And the doctor pooh-poohed it in a way but said go ahead and try it. I quit coffee and the headaches disappeared."

●

If the case of this woman were an isolated one, I could be more forgiving. But the fact of the matter is, only infrequently did doctors recommend to our group of quitters that they either cut down or quit drinking coffee—despite the fact they had been regaled with a plethora of symptomatic data which is related to coffee drinking.

Nor are our figures much different from those of studies reported earlier which showed that except in a few cases, doctors did nothing to suggest that coffee drinkers eliminate or curtail their coffee consumption.

These findings are certainly in line with those reported by Dr. John F. Greden who found doctors and clinicians rarely collect historical data from patients about their caffeine consumption despite the fact that such patients complained of anxiety neurosis, a CSN disturbance which is symptomatically almost identical to that of caffeinism.

Greden concluded by urging his colleages to begin collecting such data, particularly because if they were suffering from caffeinism, the medication they might prescribe could be contradicted by their caffeine intake.

"From the clinical perspective," Greden said, "many individuals complaining of anxiety will continue to receive substantial benefit from psychopharmacological agents. For an undetermined amount of others," he cautioned, "subtracting one drug—caffeine—may be of greater benefit than adding another."

Is Your Hospital Helping Or Hurting You?

And yet, that sort of abuse is going on all the time. Caffeine is probably the most widely consumed drug in the hospital, according to one hospital source. And the possibility is readily apparent that patients can receive sufficient caffeine to cancel, neutralize or multiply the effects of other medications the patient is taking.

One writer, for example, believed that coffee is a poor choice of beverage for the schizophrenic or psychotic patients, because caffeine could be expected to raise the patient's anxiety level.

Another doctor notes that among hospitalized patients, caffeine has been demonstrated to counteract the sedative-hypnotic effects of barbiturates. Since this neutralizing effect could initiate spiraling requests for more sleep medications, it should be considered whenever insomnia complaints are present. Subjective impressions suggest, he said, that inquiries into caffeine intake before beginning "sleeping pills" are infrequent.

Could it be that many patients are already on a drug merry-go-round that includes "uppers" like caffeine and "downers" like Librium and Valium? We'll never know just how many Americans are cancelling out the effects of these downers by excessive caffeine intake.

Likewise, those medical personnel working in mental hospitals ought to be fully aware of the effects of caffeine on mental patients. Although few studies have been conducted on such patients with regard to their caffeine consumption, it would certainly appear possible that some patients are the victim of the same sort of "uppers and downers" present in some nursing homes.

In this regard, studies have been undertaken which show that caffeine has a substantial effect on how seniors sleep—and in fact—*if* they sleep.

One study covered persons between 50 and 63 years of age. It found that just a cup or two of coffee taken before bedtime reduced sleeping time by about two hours, increased the amount of time needed to fall asleep, and doubled the number of times these patients awoke during the night.

Perhaps the doctor's medical advice, then, is apropos for *all* coffee drinkers: eliminating coffee from your diet may be the greatest single kindness you can do for your mind and body. Why not kick the habit and find out the welcome news for yourself!

13

A Big Change Is Brewing

It has been almost 17 years since the Surgeon General's office first declared that smoking is harmful to your health and ordered that cigarette makers begin admitting that fact on the cigarette pack itself.

> Warning: The Surgeon General Has Determined That Cigarette Smoking Is Harmful To Your Health.

Since the report was published, but not necessarily *because* of it, 30 million Americans have kicked the cigarette habit. Millions more carefully considered the risks and have chosen never to begin this dangerous addiction. At least 50,000,000 smokers, however, chose to ignore the research of impeccable scientific authority. They continue to puff away at levels which, without question, will earn them an earlier death.

What does it all mean?

Simply this. It takes a considerable effort to educate consumers to change their ways. Generations, in fact, may pass before the addictive use subsides. It may *never* completely disappear.

Seeds of Change

But the process has begun. And while it may take years to bring the coffee controversy to the level where the anti-smoking campaign is today, it still is moving in that direction. Just fifteen years ago, for example, cigarette manufacturers were claiming that scientific evidence that smoking was dangerous to health was "sketchy" and that no link between smoking and cancer was "proven."

These claims, empty then, are utterly vacuous now. There is absolutely no basis whatsoever for disbelieving what medical evidence has shown time after time and time: cigarette smoking is dangerous to your health.

The Growing Movement

Already, millions of coffee drinkers are kicking the habit, a fact proven by statistics provided by coffee growers themselves. But these coffee quitters are kicking the habit largely of their own volition, their own self-prescription—not by any governmental campaign or doctor's warning. But real change will occur only through programs of research, regulation, education and persuasion. And all are sadly lacking.

The Need For Research

The principal catalyst of change in the coffee controversy will no doubt flow from scientific research. A firm base of knowledge is absolutely essential to provide the information citizens must have to make their decisions wisely.

Certainly, many coffee drinkers are conducting their own research every day, as they analyze cause and effect relationships between their coffee consumption and the pathologies that follow.

But the most meaningful kind of research will take place in colleges and universities across the country, in government agencies, by medical organizations, consumer groups and by professional research organizations, both public and private.

Our area of inquiry into coffee drinking and health will have to move beyond medicine into the fields of education and behavioral science. Many unanswered questions remain about coffee drinking and health. There is some evidence, for example, that women quit drinking coffee at higher rates than men—but why? Some observers suggest that because women may be more severely harmed by coffee, they quit coffee in greater numbers. But in fact we do not know; the answers to that and other questions about coffee drinking must be pursued through future behavioral research.

Research Is Lacking

But the amount of research currently being undertaken on coffee drinking and the ailments and diseases it causes, is miniscule, to be sure. While a number of studies are currently being undertaken, they are far short of the number *needed* to provide the firm base of knowledge we see as necessary. Yes, they are far more numerous than in year's past, but far too few to be sufficient.

Still, the number is *growing*. And no doubt, it will continue to grow as the Americans become more and more concerned about what coffee is doing to their health.

What Government Is Doing

Because of the data showing caffeine to be an animal teratogen, the FDA has proposed that caffeine be *removed* from its list of substances classified as Generally Recognized As Safe (GRAS).

The GRAS list has been around since 1961 and includes some 400 substances commonly used in foods. Whether the substances on the list are, in fact, safe, is another matter and one which has not escaped FDA attention.

In 1971, the FDA contracted with FASEB (Federation of American Scientists for Experimental Biology) to undertake an examination of the GRAS list. Based upon the FASEB review, the FDA decides whether to remove the substance from the GRAS list; whether it should be allowed on a temporary basis while further studies of the substances are made, or whether the substance will be exonerated.

At the same time of the FASEB review, caffeine was allowed to temporarily remain on the GRAS list until more research is completed.

In a subsequent review of caffeine, but only caffeine in soft drinks, a near majority of a scientific committee of FASEB reported in 1978: (1) that it did not find "clear cut evidence that demonstrated that caffeine was a hazard to the public when used in beverages; (2) that "uncertainties," however, existed that warranted additional studies for determining the health implications of caffeine; and (3) that it was "inappropriate" to permit caffeine to remain on the GRAS list.[1]

Thus, the FASEB suggested that caffeine be removed from the GRAS list—and still it remains.

Removal from the GRAS list would require manufacturers to conduct still more studies to determine if there is any relationship between caffeine and human birth defects.

In addition, the FDA has proposed to change the food standard for cola and pepper drinks so that these names can be used for decaffeinated soft drinks. Currently, because caffeine is naturally present in the extracts used for cola and pepper drinks, it is a *mandatory* component for any nonartificially sweetened drink that uses the name cola and pepper. The regulation is not a well-regarded one however, because there are, in fact, non-caffeinated cola beverages on the market. Both Canada Dry and Royal Crown are producing caffeine-free colas.

The FDA announced that it will propose a change in the soft drink regulation so that cola beverages would not be required to contain caffeine. The deputy director of the Bureau of Foods, acknowledged that the change would be more form than substance noting that some cola producers have taken the cue already. But more important, removal of the restriction might well have the effect of encouraging the development of non-caffeinated colas, to replace those caffeine-laden Cokes, Pepsis, etc., now on the market.

The government also has moved, although far more slowly than many consumer groups might like, to mount an educational campaign of its own to alert women to the dangers of caffeine.

In September of 1980, after four and one-half years of meetings, petitions, a law suit and a steady stream of communication, the FDA finally agreed with consumer groups to advise pregnant women to avoid caffeine.

The FDA initiated a campaign intended to cut caffeine consumption by pregnant women and in earlier chapters, we described just some of the steps that were taken to effect that change, including warnings to doctors, medical associations and journals, government health clinics and local health departments.

Is it working? I don't know. But I expect as you might, that there remain great numbers of pregnant women out there who still are unaware of the dangers to their unborn when they drink coffee and caffeine.

But where does that leave the rest of us? Those of us who are *not* pregnant? Presently, few, if any, get warnings at all from the government.

And here again, the government could well be playing a critical role—but it is not at the present time.

What consumer groups would like to see is something like this:

Warning: The Surgeon General Has Determined That Coffee And Beverages Containing Caffeine Are Harmful To Your Health.

A warning label on coffee drawing attention to the hazards of drinking coffee and caffeine, particularly for female coffee drinkers, would stimulate health-conscious Americans into re-evaluating their coffee consumption.

The Center for Science in the Public Interest said that it has written to major coffee producers, urging them to voluntarily place a warning notice on their coffee labels. Thus far, none has picked up on the organization's suggestion, but at least one tea manufacturer has put caffeine warning labels on its non-caffeinated tea. Although many tea manufacturers state on their packaging that their teas do not contain caffeine, Health Valley, states right on the label that, not only does their tea not contain caffeine, but goes on to describe some of the harmful effects of caffeinated teas.

Education Is A Slow Process

It is one thing to be unaware of the dangers of coffee and caffeine consumption. That problem could be greatly eased by putting warning labels on these products. However, it is quite another thing to *react* upon the information once it's been disseminated.

Obviously, cigarette smokers for years have been reading, and ignoring warning labels on cigarette packs. The warning obviously is not enough. It's something. But it falls considerably short of converting great numbers of smokers to less sinful ways.

That's why the work of the consumer groups and major health organizations play such a critical role in getting the word out, as well as the media: radio, television, newspapers, magazines, books and pamphlets. They all play a tremendous part in helping Americans understand the medical dangers involved in coffee drinking and actually helping them to kick the habit.

This is the sort of thing that has occurred in cigarette smoking. After it was determined that cigarette smoking is harmful to your health, government and a wide number of health organizations undertook the educational effort to help smokers kick the habit. The American Cancer Society conducts courses on how to quit smoking and publishes millions of pamphlets and other information to help spread the message about cigarette smoking's harmful effects. The American Lung Association and the American Heart Association have undertaken similar projects.

When the coffee drinker is confronted on many sides with the truth about coffee drinking and the health dangers it presents, when he or she receives information about quitting, and when he or she finally makes a commitment for a cleaner, healthier life, "Quitting Time" will be at hand.

But unfortunately, there is less than consensus among health groups about the dangers of coffee drinking. If anything, the situation presents a mixed bag of results.

Consumer groups, as you might expect, are in the forefront of change, as they historically have been on issues which affect human health.

The Center for Science in the Public Interest has been one of the leading agitators for increased research into the coffee controversy and warning labels on products containing caffeine and increased publicity of the dangers coffee presents. Other consumer groups are following CSPI's lead.

Major health organizations, however, are worse than divided on their views—leaving an uneven picture of fragmentary support, following partisan purposes.

The March of Dimes, for example, is vitally interested in the welfare of children and thus, has taken a stand on the dangers caffeine presents to the human fetus. The Breast Cancer Advisory Center, like other health educational groups, supports the research and findings which suggest caffeine is related to breast tumors—but they have little interest in whether caffeine causes ulcers or heart disease. Other health organizations follow suit, each slicing off their chunk of the coffee controversy.

None endorse the sort of uniform condemnation so necessary for real change to take place. That sort of action will be taken only when a wide-ranging amount of research occurs that further supports that which we already know.

If you have ever read the Surgeon General's report on Smoking and Health, you've got to be impressed at the massive amount of research that was conducted before the committee reached that momentous decision that smoking is dangerous to your health.

Coffee and caffeine have generated not nearly so much critical study. Lack of research is, no doubt, the single, most important reason why consumption of these substances has been allowed to continue largely unchallenged. As more and more studies confirm what thousands of those injured by coffee already know, rapid change will begin to take place.

Additional studies will clarify the picture of coffee's harmful effects. They will show that coffee drinking at low levels, one or two cups a day, *may* be harmless, and in fact, beneficial. They will prove that drinking coffee in amounts of three or more cups can be habit forming and dangerous to your health.

Those findings—sooner or later—will compel government and the makers of these products to warn consumers through effective labeling, that coffee could ruin their health.

The ball is already rolling in that direction. As the results of new studies are released, as more books, newspaper and magazine articles are written, the truth about coffee will become clearer, more acceptable, more credible, and more catalytic to change.

It most certainly will take time, as I indicated earlier. Changes of the dramatic nature we're speaking of take years to produce. It will be *generations* before the addiction is reduced to tolerable levels, down from the epidemic proportions of the current nationwide addiction. But it *will* happen, because we're too smart not to *make* it happen.

What's most impressive is that even without massive research, millions of drinkers have found coffee so harmful that they're kicking the habit of their own volition. They need no books, no research reports, no magazine articles. They've learned that when your body *hurts*, there's something wrong—it's trying to tell you something. It's saying that coffee and caffeine are terribly bad for your body. Start trusting the signals your body gives today. Strike coffee and caffeine from your diet and start living a happier, healthier life right now.

14

Nutritious Coffee Alternatives

Even before you've given up coffee, you're likely to worry about what you're going to drink to fill that void created by its absence. This void appears larger than life, like a cavity feels to a probing tongue.

Actually, it's not nearly so difficult as you might think. And millions of quitters have found other beverages to replace coffee in their lives, some rather creatively.

You may be very surprised to learn that when most coffee drinkers kick the coffee habit they *do not* follow the cue of television's Robert Young and start drinking decaffeinated coffee. In fact, that's the *last thing* they do. And we were interested in finding out why.

Most of the coffee drinkers we questioned just couldn't conceive of returning to coffee drinking in *any* form— decaffeinated, fake, you name it.

"I can't even look at the stuff ...", one quitter told us. "It's repulsive to me. I've tried having a cup after dinner but I just can't get the stuff down."

This woman's remarks are similar to many people in our survey. Once you've kicked the coffee habit, you're just not likely to return to coffee in any guise.

Part of that reason, I suspect, is the need for a quitter to feel that he or she has really given up the dirty brew. More than one respondent said they didn't want to get into the habit of drinking decaffeinated or coffee-like substances because they feared they would revert to the real thing. And they didn't want that to happen at any cost. The situation was likened to a recovered alcoholic drinking near-beer or Catawba juice; it amounted to some wishful game-playing that could produce an opportunity to "fall off the wagon" at some later date.

What Former Coffee Drinkers Switched To When They Quit:	
Herbal Tea	37%
Water	23%
Nothing	14%
Coffee Substitutes	9%
Soft Drinks	4-1/2%
Milk, Orange Juice	4-1/2%
Decaffeinated Coffee	4-1/2%
Regular Tea	3-1/2%

But as you look over their list, it is dramatically clear that there's not a whole lot of creativity going on when it's time to find something new to drink instead of coffee. Look closely as you'll find that nearly three-fourths of the coffee quitters we questioned, switched to tea, water or nothing. Obviously, plain old water is one of the greatest elixirs known to man, but you would think we could come up with something a little more interesting than that.

The Answer May Be In Your Health Food Store

Or Well-Stocked Grocery Market

If you haven't taken the time to visit a health food store, give it a try now to get the lowdown on what's available to drink instead of coffee.

Sure, the supermarkets have a couple of items, but nobody's supermarket that we know, save the 92,000 sq. ft. Byerly's store in Minneapolis, can stock everything. Not even Byerly's does (but it comes close).

Take a walk down the aisles of your health food store and see if you aren't pleasantly amazed at all the other things there are in life to drink—besides coffee.

Herbal Teas

The myriad of caffeine-free teas available is both overwhelming and intriguing. We offer these suggestions when shopping for tea:

*Carefully Read the List of Ingredients. Most packages of tea indicate "caffeine-free" somewhere on the box or bag, although some do not. And not all herbal teas are caffeine-free. Most are, but any teas listing maté as an ingredient are not caffeine-free. *Maté is an herb which has its own caffeine.*

*Trust Your Sense Of Smell When Selecting a Tea. The combinations of herbs, flowers, and fruits that appeal to your nose will permeate the room with pleasant scents and will likely taste good as well.

*Try the Sampler Packages of Tea When Available. You'll save yourself from having boxes of disliked tea in the cupboard.

*Share Teas With Friends. New varieties can be tried without the expense of purchasing entire boxes of tea.

*Be Creative With Loose Leaf Teas. Teas come in single cup serving bags or in loose leaf form. Try mixing your own special blends.

*Look For Those Teas Which Include Your Favorite Dried Fruits, Berries and Herbs.** Some of the ingredients you can expect to find are:

Rosehips	Cinnamon
Lemon Grass	Nutmeg
Hibiscus Flowers	Roasted Barley
Peppermint Leaves	Strawberry Leaves
Orange Peel	Ginger
Apples	Spearmint
Chamomile	Ginseng
Roasted Chicory Roots	Carob
Hawthorne Berries	Citric Acid
Red Clover Blossoms	Comfrey Leaves

Here's a list of tea brands which can be found in most health food stores and well-stocked grocery markets.

Celestial Seasonings

You'll easily recognize Celestial Seasonings teas because their packages are probably the most aesthetically pleasing products on the shelf. Besides being pretty, the boxes provide information about the attributes of the tea blends, a list of ingredients, directions for preparation and inspirational quotes. (For example: "The world has lost its taste for simple things like the love of a woman for only one man."—Sophia Loren.)

Country Apple	Peppermint
Iced Delight	Emporer's Choice—with ginseng
Mandarin Orange Spice	Rosehips
Cinnamon Rose	Pelican Punch—especially for kids
Grandma's Tummy Mint	Sleepytime
Lemon Mist	Mellow Mint
Roastaroma—coffee substitute	Spearmint
Chamomile	Red Zinger
Mo's 24 Herb	

Celestial Seasonings also has an all-purpose grind international style beverage called "Breakaway." It contains no caffeine and no coffee. The flavors of "Breakaway" are Orange Cappuccino, Carob Mint and Cinnamon Splendor.

Healthway

Healthway teas are generally packaged in bulk (loose leaf) making it easy to formulate your own unusual blends. They're primarily a "one-ingredient" tea so don't look for exotic combinations of herbs and fruits.

Alfalfa Leaf	Buchu Leaf	Juniper Berry
Blueberry Leaf	Celery Leaf	Licorice Root
Buckthorn Bark	Celery Seed	Papaya Leaf
Cammomile*	Foenugreek Seed	Raspberry Leaf
Catnip	Golden Rod	Hawthorn Berry
Rosemary	Comfrey Leaf	Hyssop Herb
Valarian Root	Comfrey Root	Dulse Leaves
Cypress Sage	Dandelion Leaf	Linden Flower
Cleavers	Dandelion Root	Scullcap
Parsley	Elderflower Tea	Rose Hip Powder
Uva Ursi	Couch Grass	
Sarsaparilla	Eyebright	

*Webster's New World Dictionary defines chamomile as a plant whose dried, daisylike flower heads have been used in a medicinal tea. The preferred spelling is "chamomile." Processors are at their whim when spelling teas so you'll likely see a variety of spellings.

Alvita

Alvita tea packages are duller than most but they provide tea-making directions and a list of the ingredients.

Couchgrass	Alfalfa Leaf
Alfalfa Peppermint Leaf	Papaya Mint

Alvita (cont.)

Fennel Seed

Chaparral

Chia

Hops

Huckleberry Leaf

Watermelon Seed

Papaya Leaf

Strawberry Leaf

Shavegrass

Scullcap

Senna Leaf

Parsley

Health Valley

Health Valley believes that just as we don't eat the same foods at every meal, neither should we drink the same tea all day. The boxes give "how to" information about the blending of herb teas and a list of ingredients.

Natural Morning Herb Tea

Natural Daytime Herb Tea

Natural Evening Herb Tea

Magic Mountain

Magic Mountain boxes look like brightly decorated miniature Kleenex boxes. There is a list of ingredients on each package.

Peppermint Spice

Sweet Apple Spice

Sweet Cinnamon Spice

Morning Sun

Sweet Almond

Wild Red Mint

Sweet Orange Spice

Bigelow

Bigelow tea boxes are recognized by the appealing photographs of a bicyclist or hang glider, and nature scenes. The ingredients are listed on each box.

Take-A-Break

Sweet Dreams

Mint Medley

Feeling Free

Nice Over Ice

Apple Orchard

Looking Good

Lipton

Lipton is the grand master of teas yet they have few varieties of herbal, caffeine-free teas. The ingredients are listed on each box.

Toasty Spice	Almond Pleasure
Gentle Orange	Quietly Chamomile
Red Hibiscus	

Instant Drinks

Instant drinks are not only a tasty alternative to caffeinated beverages, but are often nutritious and can double as a quick meal on occasion. They can be mixed strictly as directed or with a little creativity, you can add such ingredients as juices, fruits, yogurt or ice cream. Best of all, instant drinks can be prepared hot or cold so if you're looking for a completely new morning "pick me up", this could be it!

Richlife

Richlife is a natural protein drink, "a meal." It has 220 calories and comes in a ready-to-drink-from can.

CaraCoa

CaraCoa is an instant carob drink that has a taste similar to chocolate. There is no caffeine or chocolate in CaraCoa.

Caroba

Caroba is an instant carob drink which is sweetened with fructose and has no chocolate or caffeine.

NuLife

NuLife is an instant lemon-flavored drink mix. It is sweetened with fructose and has 1,000 mg of vitamin C per serving.

Tisa

Tisa comes in beverage cube form and is made from dried extracts, vitamin C and turbinado sugar. A one-cup serving has 28 calories. The flavors are Rose Hip, Chamomile, Peppermint, and Fruit.

Fruit Juices

For nearly every fruit, there's a nectar to match. Fruit juices are colorful, healthful and readily available. They're also a great source of natural sweetener to be used in recipes or with other beverages. Fruit juices are packaged in bottles (plastic and glass), frozen containers and cans.

Here's what you'll likely find in your health food market.

R.W. Knudsen Family
R.W. Knudsen Family juices have no added sugars and come in non-carbonated and "sparkling" form.

Tangerine	Apple-Lime
Very Veggie	Apple Raisin
Apple-Cranberry	Cider and Spice
Pina Colada	

Mission San Juan
Mission San Juan juices have no added sweeteners. Their juices are non-carbonated.

Grape	Apple Cranberry
Honey Lemon	Apple 'n Spice
Nectar	

Hansen's
Hansen's juices are unfiltered and have no added sweeteners.

Strawberry Nectar	Papaya Juice
Apple	Pinneapple-Coconut

Hain
Hain juices are primarily ready to drink but also come in a concentrate form. The juices may have honey added as a sweetener.

Strawberry	Apricot
Apple	Red Raspberry

Hain (cont.)

Cranberry Cocktail	Celery Juice
Carrot	Beet Juice
Natural Vegetable Cocktail	Cabbage Juice

Hawaiian Sun

Hawaiian Sun juices may have sugar or corn sweetener added.

Papaya	Pineapple Nectar
Guava Nectar	

Mineral Waters

For many people, tap water is the best thing to cool a hardy thirst. Witness the fact that almost one-fourth of our coffee quitters switched to water. But for others, tap water is just plain old dull. Bottled mineral water can provide these tap-water weary drinkers with an interesting and healthful alternative to caffeinated beverages.

Bottled waters vary in price, origin, flavor and levels of carbonation. You'll find bottled mineral waters in health food stores, grocery markets and in liquor stores. We suggest trying several waters before deciding whether or not this is a drink you will like. Here's a list of some of the brands of bottled water and where they originate.

Cold Spring—Wisconsin	Vichy—France
Bartlett—California	San Pellegrino—Italy
Perrier—France	Evian—France
Apollinaris—Germany	Canada Dry Club Soda—
Poland Spring—Maine	Bottled regionally
Mountain Valley—Arkansas	

Health Food Soda

Health food soda or pop is a canned carbonated beverage with no caffeine. The soda is usually sweetened with honey or fructose.

Health Valley
Rootbeer
Ginger Ale
Grape

Richlife Nutri-Pop—multivitamin supplement
Lemon-Lime
Rootbeer
Cola
Blackberry

Hansen's
Mandarin Lime
Lemon Lime

Coffee Substitutes

For those of you who simply cannot live without the taste of coffee, or the look of coffee in your cup, there are some coffee substitutes which contain no coffee and no caffeine. Be advised, however, that some researchers have found that *any* beverage which is made from *roasted* grains or beans may be a co-carcinogen or at worst, a carcinogen. My advice, is that if you're going to quit coffee—*Quit Coffee.* But you be the judge.

We found four major brands of coffee substitutes and they all contained similar ingredient combinations: roasted barley, rye, chicory, shredded beet roots.

Pionier—Instant Swiss Coffee Substitute, Switzerland
Pero—Instant Cereal Beverage, Germany
Cafix—Natural Cereal Beverage, West Germany
Duram—Un-Coffee, in perk or drip form, California

A Parting Thought

There is something about a health food store that conjures up among some people, visions of dull, lifeless food which, like medicine, must taste awful because it's supposed to be good for you.

Just as bad, if you actually enjoy eating these foods, you'll instantly develop the image of an intolerant health food proselyte who seeks to convert the ignorant masses from Cokes, coffee and "Big Macs" to the "good life" of lentils, sprouts, brewers yeast and blackstrap molasses.

And that's too bad. Because neither vision is accurate, although in honesty, both have some basis in fact, albeit remarkably slim.

Health food stores are actually pretty interesting places to learn something about the food you're dumping into the caloric burner and about how to live a happier, healthier life.

The point I'm trying to make is that when you start stocking up on health food store alternatives to coffee, be prepared for some chiding from your less food-conscious friends. Never mind they eat all those junk foods which are high in refined sugar, starch, white flour and above all else—caffeine. When you switch to Perrier, be ready because somebody's going to rib you about drinking "snob water."

Ask your restaurant waitress for one of the instant carob drinks and if she's a coffee drinker, she'll look at you like you're some highfalutin wiseacre. Then she'll pass on one of those holier than thou looks and offer black coffee.

So get used to (1) stocking up on your favorite alternatives from the health food store while you duck the ribbing from well-meaning friends; (2) doing without when you're at a restaurant or a friend's house; (3) suffering the embarrassment of saying "no thank you" to coffee and saying "I'll just have water instead."

The payoff, though, is pretty important. You're going to live a healthier life when you decide to kick the coffee habit. And if you follow our health food store suggestions, you'll no doubt find drinks which are far more healthy, more nutritious, and in all likelihood, much better tasting.

And that's going to make you a *winner* in everybody's book, including mine.

Good luck and long life!

Daily Caffeine Log

Day _____   Date _____

Time	Product	Ounces	Milligrams
____	____	____	____
____	____	____	____
____	____	____	____
____	____	____	____
____	____	____	____
____	____	____	____
____	____	____	____
____	____	____	____
____	____	____	____
____	____	____	____
____	____	____	____
____	____	____	____
____	____	____	____
____	____	____	____
____	____	____	____
____	____	____	____

Daily Caffeine Log

Day _____   Date _____

Time	Product	Ounces	Milligrams
_____	_____	_____	_____
_____	_____	_____	_____
_____	_____	_____	_____
_____	_____	_____	_____
_____	_____	_____	_____
_____	_____	_____	_____
_____	_____	_____	_____
_____	_____	_____	_____
_____	_____	_____	_____
_____	_____	_____	_____
_____	_____	_____	_____
_____	_____	_____	_____
_____	_____	_____	_____
_____	_____	_____	_____
_____	_____	_____	_____

Daily Caffeine Log

Day _____   Date _____

Time	Product	Ounces	Milligrams
————	————	————	————
————	————	————	————
————	————	————	————
————	————	————	————
————	————	————	————
————	————	————	————
————	————	————	————
————	————	————	————
————	————	————	————
————	————	————	————
————	————	————	————
————	————	————	————
————	————	————	————
————	————	————	————
————	————	————	————
————	————	————	————

Daily Caffeine Log

Day _____   Date _____

Time	Product	Ounces	Milligrams
____	____	____	____
____	____	____	____
____	____	____	____
____	____	____	____
____	____	____	____
____	____	____	____
____	____	____	____
____	____	____	____
____	____	____	____
____	____	____	____
____	____	____	____
____	____	____	____
____	____	____	____
____	____	____	____
____	____	____	____
____	____	____	____

Daily Caffeine Log

Day _____   Date _____

Time	Product	Ounces	Milligrams
___	___	___	___
___	___	___	___
___	___	___	___
___	___	___	___
___	___	___	___
___	___	___	___
___	___	___	___
___	___	___	___
___	___	___	___
___	___	___	___
___	___	___	___
___	___	___	___
___	___	___	___
___	___	___	___
___	___	___	___
___	___	___	___

Daily Caffeine Log

Day _____   Date _____

Time	Product	Ounces	Milligrams
_____	_____	_____	_____
_____	_____	_____	_____
_____	_____	_____	_____
_____	_____	_____	_____
_____	_____	_____	_____
_____	_____	_____	_____
_____	_____	_____	_____
_____	_____	_____	_____
_____	_____	_____	_____
_____	_____	_____	_____
_____	_____	_____	_____
_____	_____	_____	_____
_____	_____	_____	_____
_____	_____	_____	_____
_____	_____	_____	_____
_____	_____	_____	_____

Daily Caffeine Log

Day _____   Date _____

Time	Product	Ounces	Milligrams
_____	_____	_____	_____
_____	_____	_____	_____
_____	_____	_____	_____
_____	_____	_____	_____
_____	_____	_____	_____
_____	_____	_____	_____
_____	_____	_____	_____
_____	_____	_____	_____
_____	_____	_____	_____
_____	_____	_____	_____
_____	_____	_____	_____
_____	_____	_____	_____
_____	_____	_____	_____
_____	_____	_____	_____
_____	_____	_____	_____
_____	_____	_____	_____

Daily Caffeine Log

Day _____   Date _____

Time	Product	Ounces	Milligrams
____	____	____	____
____	____	____	____
____	____	____	____
____	____	____	____
____	____	____	____
____	____	____	____
____	____	____	____
____	____	____	____
____	____	____	____
____	____	____	____
____	____	____	____
____	____	____	____
____	____	____	____
____	____	____	____
____	____	____	____
____	____	____	____

Notes

Chapter One

1. Data Group, Inc., Elkins, Penn. *Summary of National Coffee Drinking Survey, Winter 1980.* Prepared for the National Coffee Association of the U.S.A., Inc.
2. National Center for Health Statistics, Washington, D.C. *Use Habits Among Adults of Cigarettes, Coffee, Aspirin, and Sleeping Pills, United States.* 1976. U.S. Department of Health, Education and Welfare.
3. *Ibid.*

Chapter Two

1. Merritt, M.C. and Proctor, B.E.: *Effects of Temperature during the roasting cycle on selected components of different types of whole bean coffee.* Food Research 22: 222, 1957.
2. Clementa, R.S., and Deatherage, F.E.: *A chromatagraphic study of some of the compounds in roasted coffee.* Food Research 22: 222, 1957.
3. *World Book Encyclopedia*, Coffee, page 606.
4. *Ibid.*

Notes—Chapter Two (cont.)

5. Norman Kolpas, *The Coffee Lovers' Companion.*
6. John F. Greden, *Coffee, Tea and You.* The Sciences, January 1979. Page 6.
7. John Svicarovich, Stephen Winter, Jeff Ferguson, *The Coffee Book.* Page 10-11.
8. *Ibid.*
9. *Ibid.*
10. Ritchie, J.M. *Central Nervous System Stimulants.* The xanthines. In Goodman, L.S. and Gilman, A., eds.: The Pharmacological Basis of Therapeutics, 4th ed. N.Y.: Macmillan Co. 1970.
11. Truitt, E.B., Jr.: The Xanthines. In DiPalma, J.R., ed.: *Drill's Pharmacology in Medicine.* 4th ed. N.Y.: McGraw-Hill Book Co., Inc., 1971.
12. Stanley R. Newman, Letter to Editor, Cocoa and Caffeine, The Sciences, Oct. 1979. Page 3
13. *Nutrition Action,* newsletter published by Center for Science in the Public Interest, 1755 S Street, N.W., Washington, D.C. 20009.

Chapter Three

1. National Center for Health Statistics, Washington, D.C. *Use Habits Among Adults of Cigarettes, Coffee, Aspirin, and Sleeping Pills, United States.* 1976. U.S. Department of Health, Education and Welfare.
2. Data Group, Inc., Elkins, Penn. *Summary of National Coffee Drinking Survey, Winter 1980.* Prepared for the National Coffee Association of the U.S.A., Inc.
3. *Ibid.*
4. Chris Lecos, FDA Consumer, October 1980, Page 6.
5. *Ibid.*
6. National Center for Health Statistics, Washington, D.C. *Use Habits Among Adults of Cigarettes, Coffee, Aspirin, and Sleeping Pills, United States.* 1976. U.S. Department of Health, Education and Welfare.
7. Data Group, Inc., Elkins, Penn. *Summary of National Coffee Drinking Survey, Winter, 1980.* Prepared for the National Coffee Association of the U.S.A., Inc.

Chapter Four
1. National Center for Health Statistics, Washington D.C.

Chapter Five
1. Brecher, E.C.: *Licit and Illicit Drugs: The Consumers Union Report on Narcotics, Stimulants, Depressants, Inhalants, Hallucinogens and Marijuana—including Caffeine, Nicotine and Alcohol.* Boston: Little, Brown & Co., Inc. 1972.
2. Jokela, S. and Varliainen, A., *Caffeine poisoning,* Acta Phamacol. Toxicol. 15 (1959) 331-334.
3. DiMaio, V.J.M. and Garriott, J.C.: *Lethal Caffeine Poisoning in a Child,* Forensic Science 3 (1974) 279-281.
4. E. Grusz-Hardy, *Lethal caffeine poisoning,* Bull. Int. Assoc. Forens. Toxicol. April (1973) 6-7.
5. Alstott, R.L., Miller, A.J. and Forney, R.B.: *Report of a human fatality due to caffeine,* J. Forens, Sci. 18 (1973) 135-137.
6. Greden, J.F.: *Coffee, Tea and You,* The Sciences, January 1979, 6-11.
7. *Ibid,* Greden, J.F.
8. Mueller-Limmroth, W.: *Der Einfluss von coffeinhaltigem und coffeinfreiem Kasffee auf den Schlaf des Menschen.* Z. Ernahrungswiss. 14: Suppl. 14, 1972. P. 46.
9. Schwertz, M.T. and Marbach, G.: *Effets Physiologiques de lo cafeine et du meprobamate au cours du sommeil chez l'homme.* Arch. Sci. Physiol. 19: 425, 1965.
10. Goldstein, A., Warren JR., and Kaizer, S.: *Psychotropic effects on caffeine in man. 1. Individual differences in sensitivity to caffeine-induced wakefulness.* J. Pharmacol. Exp. Ther. 149: 156, 1965. Goldstein, A., *Wakefulness caused by caffeine.* Naunyn-Schmiedeberg, Arch. Exp. Pat. 248. 269, 1964.
11. Greden, J.F.: *Anxiety or Caffeinism: A Diagnostic Dilemma.* American Journal of Psychiatry, 1974, 131, 1089-1092.
12. MacCallum, W.A. Gordon, *Excess Coffee and Anxiety States,* International Journal of Social Psychiatry, 1979, 25 (3) 209.
13. Verner Stillner, M.D., M.P.H., Michale K. Popkin, M.D., and Chester M. Pierce, M.D. *Caffeine-Induced Delirium During Prolonged Competitive Stress,* American Journal of Psychiatry, 135:7 July 1978.

Chapter Six

1. MacMahon, Brian, M.D., Yen, Stella, M.D., Trichopolous, Dimitrio, M.D., and Nardi, George, M.D., *Coffee and Cancer of the Pancreas,* New England Journal of Medicine, March 12, 1981.
2. Lin R.S., Kessler, II. *A Multifactorial Model for Pancreatic Cancer in Man; Epidemiologic Evidence.* Journal of the American Medical Association, 1981; 245: 147-52.
3. Lecos, Chris, FDA Consumer, May 1980.
4. Williams, Dr. Kenneth, *Prevention,* April 1980.
5. Rehn, L. *Blasengeschwultste Bein Anitinarteiten.* Arch Klin Chir 1895; 50: 558-600.
6. Howe, G.R., Burch, J.D., Miller, A.B., Cook, G.M., Esteve, J., Morrison, B., Gordon, P., Chambers, L.W., Fodor, G. and Winsor, G.M., *Tobacco Use, Occupation, Coffee, Various Nutrients and Bladder Cancer.* JNCI, Vol 64. No. 4, April, 1980.

Chapter Seven

1. DiMaio, V.J.M. and Farriott, J.C., *Lethal Caffeine Poisoning In A Child.* Forensic Science 3 (1974) 275-278.
2. Boston Collaborative Drug Surveillance Program, *Coffee Drinking and Acute Myocardial Infarction.* Lancet 1972-II 1278 (1973).
3. The Framingham Study: *An epidemiological investigation of cardiovascular disease.* Section 26. Edited by WM Kannel, T. Gordon. Washington, D.C. Government Printing Office. 1970.
4. Heyden, S., Heyden, F., Heiss, G. Hames, C.G. *Smoking and Coffee Consumptior 'n Three Groups: Cancer Deaths, Cardiovascular Deaths and Living Controls. A Prospective Study in Evans County, Georgia.* J. Chron Dis. Vo. 32, PP. 673-677.
5. Paul, O. Postgra Med. 44 196 (1968)
6. Heyden, S., Tyroler, Herman A., Heiss, G. Hames, Curtis, G., and Bartel, Alan. *Coffee Consumption and Mortality.* Arch Intern Med. Vol 138. Oct. 1978.

Chapter Eight

1. Roth, J.S., Ivy, A.C., and Atkinson, A.J. *Caffeine and "Peptic" Ulcer. Relation of Caffeine and Caffeine-Containing Beverages to Pathogenesis, Diagnosis and Management of the "Peptic" Ulcer.* Journal of the American Medical Association. 126: 814, 1944.

Notes—Chapter Eight (cont.)

2. Cohen, S., M.D. *Pathogenesis of Coffee-Induced Gastrointestinal Symptoms*. New England Journal of Medicine. Vol. 303 N. 3 July 17, 1980.

3. *Ibid.*

4. Thomas, Fred B., Steinbaugn, Jan. T. Fromkes, John J., Mekhjian Hagop S., and Caldwell, James H., *Inhibitory Effect of Coffee on Lower Esophageal Sphincter Pressure*. Gastroenterology 79: 1262-1266, 1980.

Chapter Nine

1. Science Information File, March of Dimes Birth Defects Foundatiion, September 1980.

2. Collins, TFX, Welsh, J.W., Black, T.C., and Collins, E.V., *A comprehensive study of the teratogenic potential of caffeine in rats when given by oral intubation*. J. Environ. Toxicol. and Pathol, in press; preprint included in Report on Caffeine, DFA. (Sept) 1980.

3. News Release. Published by Center for Science in the Public Interest, 1755 S Street N.W., Washington, D.C., 20009.

4. *Ibid.*

5. Patwardhan, R.V., Desmond, P.V., Johnson, Raymond F., and Schenker, Steven. *Impaired Elimination of Caffeine By Oral Contraceptive Steroids*. Journal of Lab. Clin. Med. April 1980.

6. FDA Drug Bulletin, Vol. 10, Number 3. Public Health Service, November 1980.

7. Op. Cit. Patwardhan et. al.

8. Surgeon General's Advisory Committee: *Smoking and Health* (Pub. No. 1103) United States Public Health Service, Washington, D.C., 1964.

9. Minton, John P., M.D. Foecking, M.D., Webster, D.J.T., Ch. B., F.R.C.S. and Matthews, R.H., Ph.D. *Caffeine, Cyclic Nucleotides, and Breast Disease*. Surgery 1979.

10. Op. Cit. *Nutrition Action.*

11. *Ibid.*

Chapter Ten

1. Smith, Lee, *A Superpower Enters The Soft-Drink Wars*, Fortune, June 30, 1980.

2. Bunker, Mary Louise and McWilliams, Margaret, *Caffeine Content of Common Beverages,* Journal of the American Dietetic Assn. Vol. 74, 1979.

3. Silver, W., *Insomnia, Tachicardia, and Cola Drinks, Pediatrics,* 47: 635, 1971.

Chapter Eleven

1. Ferguson, Tom, M.D., Graedon, Joe, M.A., *Caffeine,* Medical Self-Care, Winter 1980.

2. Bunker, Mary Louise and McWilliams, Margaret, *Caffeine Content of Common Beverages,* Journal of American Dietetic Association, Vol. 74, January 1979.

Chapter Twelve

1. Lecos, Chris, *Caution Light on Caffeine, FDA Consumer, October 1980.*

Index